Living Multiple Lifestyles in One Lifetime
an

Dr. Delowiesa Wesson

CLF Publishing, LLC.
9161 Sierra Ave, Ste. 203C
Fontana, CA 92335
www.clfpublishing.org

Copyright © 2017 by Delowiesa Wesson. All rights reserved. No portion of this book may be reproduced, stored in a retrieval system, or transmitted by any form or any means electronically, photocopied, recorded, or any other except for brief quotations in printed reviews, without the prior permission of the publisher.

All rights reserved. No portion of this book may be reproduced, stored in a retrieval system, or transmitted by any form or any means electronically, photocopied, recorded, or any other except for brief quotations in printed reviews, without the prior permission of the publisher.

Cover Design by Senir Design. Contact information- info@senirdesign.com.

ISBN # 978-1-945102-24-0

Printed in the United States of America.

DEDICATIONS

I thank God for His Son, Jesus Christ and for the mighty blessing of you, my readers.

"I dedicate this book to you; you are not alone."

I know what it feels like to be the black sheep or the child that takes the blame. I know what it feels like to be the child that was constantly talked about, laughed at, and overlooked. The child that always had to defend him/herself, because everyone was too busy to listen. That strong child that was unnoticed because of a sickly child. I know what you feel. I know what it feels like to be molested, abused, raped, teased, and mistreated. I know what it feels like to tell the truth and still be called a liar. I know what it feels like!

Lastly but definitely not least, I dedicate this book to you, the survivor, the overcomer and the suffering. You were the one in mind as I was writing. I am talking to you- the warrior, the innocent child, man or woman who had to endure. You are an overcomer and now you are walking in victory.

To the suffering, I pray you uncover, discover, and face your demons. Move on. It is your turn to live and tell your story. #catchabreak

This is your season!

ACKNOWLEDGEMENTS

*I would be remiss if I failed to acknowledge the late Reverend Dr. William H. Wofford, and I acknowledge the prophetic Word of God I received that day he called me into his office. It was around 1974 when Dr. Wofford called me to his office. One Sunday, I went to church and was singing in the choir when it was evident I was high, and yes, I was. Dr. Wofford called me into his office, and the love in Dr. Wofford's voice captivated my attention. As I listened to God's voice, the words Dr. Wofford spoke were sobering. He told me God was preparing me for generations to come and what He is allowing is for me to glorify Him. He told me I was going to be a minister of the Gospel, and I would break **new** ground for God to deliver. Then, he said, "Be encouraged, Jesus is raising a mighty warrior to be used by Him." He reassured me I was in God's care and released me to be great for God.*

I too acknowledge the inspiration God gave Bishop George A. Todd who a decade or so ago suggested I write my life's story. Thank you, Bishop Todd, for your never-ending love, patience, perseverance and encouragement to press on. I appreciate that.

I acknowledge the support of my family, large and small, near or far, for your love and support.

To my sponsors and contributors: Delores Lambert, Laurie & Johnny, La'Shawn & Rodney, Emanuel, Penny, James P., Da'jah, Jessen, Lashawnae, Jhamier, Kairo, Della and James Fuller. Gilbert Nelson, Rochelle & Anthony Oliver, Brenda Clark, Tracy & Kevin Hill, thank you!

Thank you, Dr. Claudette "Lawdy Mrs. Claudie" Williams, Emanuel, Della, Dr. C. White-Elliott, and Brenda Jones for reading and editing this material. And to all whose names I did not mention, count it to my brain, not my heart because you are always in my heart, and I thank you!

And to Dr. C. White-Elliott of CLF Publishing, without you none of this could have happened. Thank you!

It may sound strange, but I thank the contributors of the past. Yes, the abuser, molester, rapist, the ones who made this story my autobiography. You are forgiven. Godspeed!

I acknowledge the power of God in my life. Thank you, Heavenly Father, for allowing this, your servant to complete and publish, the wondrous works you have and continue to perform in my life. Thank you Jesus, for loving me and saving me from myself when I was so unlovable, and I thank you Holy Ghost, for leading and guiding me along this pilgrimage called life. Thank you, Lord!

Main characters in this chapter of my life:

Centered: mom Delores Lambert in the middle, from left to right: my big brother Gilbert, me, my Daddy, the late Gibbs Wesson, Big Momma, the late Mable Provost, my first love, the late Larry Lusby, me & my first husband, the late, Willie B. Sanders

Although there are no pictures of the Rollins or Lil' Grandma, they are here in heart! Superintendent James P. Rollins III, Uncle Rev., the late Dr. James P. Rollins II, the late Leo, Harry & Sam Rollins, Lil' Grandmother, the late Evelyn Lane

TABLE OF CONTENTS

Chapter One	9
Chapter Two	17
Chapter Three	29
Chapter Four	37
Chapter Five	41
Chapter Six	49
Chapter Seven	55
Chapter Eight	67
Chapter Nine	71
Words to …	83
God's Chair	85
References	86

Chapter One
Prelude and Introductions

My name is Delowiesa Wesson, and I have lived multiple life*styles* in one lifetime. I was born May 6, 1953, to Gibbs Wesson, of Little Rock, Arkansas, and Delores Provost, of Lake Charles, Louisiana. I was born and raised in Los Angeles, California (L.A.); however, at some point in my infancy, the family moved to Tacoma, Washington. And, that is where my story begins.

My family make-up consists of Cherokee Indian, Caucasian, and Black. My genealogy consists of the Drakes, Provosts, and Wessons, and although we have come a long way from times of slavery, it is not so distant for me. Both my grandmothers were slaves. Lil' Grandmother, my daddy's mom, was a house slave in Arkansas, and Big Momma, my mother's mom, was a slave on Lavert Plantation in Louisiana. Big Momma, Mable Drake Provost, lived in Louisiana and Lil' Grandma, Evelyn Lane Wesson, lived in Arkansas.

My very first memory is of snow, snowballs, and a huge, heavy wooden door. I recall throwing a snowball at my mom, and she retaliated by giving me a snow bath. She then taught my brother Gilbert and me how to make snow angels. We were living in Tacoma, Washington at that time. After playing, eating, and settling down for the evening, I remember sitting by a big, heavy wooden door. I would sit by that door until a tall man opened it. That man would swoop me up and throw me in the air, where I always landed on his lips. While kissing and biting my cheeks, he tickled me as he wrapped his long arms around me, giving me what he called the "Granddaddy's Bear Hug." Afterwards, he slung me onto his hip, and there I stayed.

He would sit me on his lap as he ate dinner, always sneaking me a taste of dessert.

After dinner, like clockwork, he would put me in my crib (I was about 20 to 22 months old), while he settled down for the evening. Afterwards, he would come get me, and we would go to the couch where he would kick his legs up in his comfy chair and cradle me in his arms until I fell asleep. I remember him tenderly kissing my cheek, whispering, "See you tomorrow, sweetie," as my mother took me out of his arms and tucked me into bed. That man was my grandfather, my mother's dad.

I then recall crying and crying and crying at that door. My grandmother would pull me away and set me on her knee, but I refused to stay. She would take me to the couch, but I always made my way back to the door. My mother also tried to console me but to no avail. Granddaddy had passed, no more tall man. *Where was he?* I wondered, as I wept. He no longer walked through the door and swooped me up. I knew nothing of death, but for a long time thereafter, there were only memories of crying, hurt, and pain.

Big Momma and my mom told me I stopped eating and cried myself into a state of listlessness. Momma took me to a doctor, and the doctor told her I was grief stricken and had stopped thriving, and the degree of grief was severe. Grandmomma told me the doctors suggested a simple change of scenery, suggesting the family take a vacation. "VACATION" …naw…my family moved to Los Angeles, California, where I recovered. While there, Uncle Rev., my mother's brother, graduated from Pepperdine University. That was during the mid-50s or early 60s.

Uncle Rev. was a Baptist minister and started a family-oriented church. Uncle Rev. was the founder and pastor of

Christian Missionary Baptist Church, located on 51st Street and Figueroa, in Los Angeles, California, where the building yet stands. We were at the church every day! My grandmother was the mother of the church, and we were there daily, praying with her, or at choir practice, Bible study, Mother's Board or Deacons and Deaconess meeting, church meeting, Trustee Board meeting, Mission meeting, cleaning or doing something.

Also, Uncle Rev. was the principal at Russell Elementary School where daily after school my brother, first cousins, and I went to skate, play tether ball, and hand ball. We had so much fun. During those times, we served the Lord with gladness. We truly loved hard, played hard, prayed a lot, and ate well. We wanted for nothing although according to societal standards, we were in a middle-class category. However, in our world, we were rich in houses and land, wanting for nothing. We did not know the difference between being rich or poor, high class or low class. We knew nothing of the elite. All we knew was we were the Chosen, and that was good enough for us.

When I was a child in Los Angeles, it was not as developed as it is today. I have memories of walking to the Haunted House on Sunset and Vine from 41st and Central. We used to skate to the Coliseum and play there all day long, making it home just in time for "Street Lights No Punches." Remember that? We were not far from Downtown Los Angeles, and every month, we rode the Central bus, Number 12 to Grand Central Market and Clifton's.

Thus far, I have mentioned several family members in these first few pages. Let me officially introduce you to the family. I will start with my mother and father.

My Momma*, Delores *aka Ole' Lady, Momz

My mother is with me today, and she is a feisty ole' lady, who loves the Lord. As a child, my mother worked several jobs to provide for my brother and me. She worked as a print press operator. Then, she started working for Mattel Toy Company. I had every new doll they made before it hit the market. That is probably why I collect dolls today. I had the very first Ken, Barbie, and Chatty Cathy dolls. Oh, how I loved my Chatty Cathy. She talked to me, and she listened when I spoke.

I also recall Momma working two jobs for a while. Nonetheless, there came a time when Momma started working at Rocket Cleaners on Crenshaw Boulevard where she met Lorraine Sims...another chapter of my life with her son Vincent. Momma's final job was driving a school bus for Los Angeles Unified School District (LAUSD). Every day, I prayed for the children on her route. Momma is no joke; she will check a child in a "hot" quick minute! I have seen her snatch up one of mine, and before I realized what was happening, she had the child in her grips, as she chastised her (and that was her favorite...her first-born grandchild). My baby was so startled that her eyes were as big as golf balls, and she was gasping for air.

Yet, as a young child, I remember Momz taking us to a place where loud music played. There were people dancing, smoking, drinking, laughing, and having a good time. When we got there, we were taken upstairs to a room where we watched television. I remember the room was pastel green, and there was a ceiling fan that intrigued me. That place was the 54 Ballroom, a popular nightclub during that era. However, one of the tender memories I have of Momz is going to the bowling alley with her. She loved bowling and has always been in leagues, and I remember her taking us to games, practice, or just to have fun. I remember her helping me throw a humongous, heavy ball down the aisle. My balls usually rolled right into the gutter, and still do sometimes, but Momma would always tell me, "You'll get better with practice." That one statement has been with me all my life. Momma encouraged and empowered me with hope, and that alone was all I needed to hold on to. While at the bowling alley, we could bowl and eat all the hot dogs, hamburgers and French fries we wanted. They were free to us. That was life as I knew it for quite some time.

When I was a little girl, I was a tomboy and a daydreamer, who was molested and abused. With the challenges I faced, I learned to escape mentally, emotionally, and spiritually. In doing so, I created a fairytale land where my Little Peoples and I ruled. I have many good memories of me and my Little Peoples, but those memories were superimposed upon me and combined with the breaching of my spirit to multiple degrees. However, during those times, my Little Peoples assisted me in zoning-out, and that was my coping mechanism well into adulthood.

I have learned as parents, we do our best, and just as I was a young mother, so was my mother, and yes, she made mistakes. What mother hasn't? I thank God that I have a God-fearing, wise, hard-working, loving, sincere, and dedicated mother. She is far from perfect, but so are we. Thank you, Momma, for doing your best. Thank you, Momma, for not taking a coat hanger and aborting us. Thank you, for not deserting us. Thank you, Momma, for being you and doing all you knew to do. Momma, all is well!

One thing I do know is my momma did her best! I cannot blame her for all that happened to me. ⁱHell, when the molestation and abuse started, she was a young, abused wife of the 50s. Times were much different than they are now. Today, an abused wife has rights. Back then, wives had the right to "keep their mouths shut, or get slapped, or worse." Women had no voice!

Through all my mother's hurt and pain, she never took it out on my brother or me. Momma took good care of us and was there for us. She was a hard worker, a reliable mother, a medic caring for Gilbert 24/7/365, a loving and caring daughter, sister, auntie, wife, and employee. She is so lovable and cuddly, and she has a personality that will make you take inventory of yourself. She points out a person's shortcomings or faults through love and understanding- for the most part. Well, my family knows what I mean. Momma is something else; you can always tell when Momz does not like something or when she is about to get in your business. She has gestures and murmurings that are very distinguished. Sometimes, she will have you laughing so hard that you admit your shortcomings and apologize. On the other hand, she can get a person so riled up and ready to defend him/herself at all cost; no questions asked. That lady is something else.

Momma and Daddy

I remember a picture of Momz and Dad's wedding. Momma was in a beautiful white, silk wedding dress with a long, flowing train; Daddy was all decked out in his white tuxedo with tails. They looked like the dream couple. I used to fantasize that we had a fairytale life with Mom and Dad, and our family was the Ozzie and Harriet of the community. *That was a joke!*

Gibbs, my Daddy

My daddy is deceased, and I am and always will be a "Daddy's Girl." I know little about daddy's upbringing and childhood, but I knew his mom, Evelyn Wesson Lane and step-dad, Willie Lane. We called Evelyn, Lil' Grandma because she was short and petite. I learned during my research, Daddy was an at-risk youth and gave Lil' Grandmamma trouble. He was what they called "a troubled child" and "juvenile delinquent." Due to Daddy's rebellious behavior, Grandma sent Daddy to Compton, CA, to live with relatives, Nancy and Nig Moore. Somewhere around that time, Momz and Dad met. It was around Momz' senior year, and after graduation, Momz and Dad were married. Shortly thereafter, they got pregnant with my brother, Gilbert, and a year and four months later, I was delivered into this crazy, loving, dysfunctional, God-fearing and wonderful family.

I have a total of five sisters and four brothers. My oldest sister was conceived by a woman with whom my mother went to school, and all we know is her name: Carolyn. Her family disallowed Daddy any further contact, so we never got to meet or know her. We also have an older brother, Darryl. We know Darryl, but he is an isolator and after Daddy passed, Darryl fell off the face of the earth. His daughter does not even know where he is the last time I spoke with her. Daddy remarried and had my sister Veniece. He remarried again and had Tametria, Watasha, and my knucklehead brother Javier. My sisters and I are close, except for Veniece, who has disconnected herself as well. I have also learned there are mental and or emotional deficiencies they may be faced with.

My brother Gilbert and I have the same mother, and Momma had her hands full with Gilbert, who was sickly with childhood asthma. When Daddy was around, he cared for me. I was his Little Princess "Cookie," and he spoiled me as every doting father loves and spoils his daughter. Daddy branded me with the nickname "Cookie." He said when I was born I had little brown freckles all over and a round face that reminded him of his favorite cookie "Cholate Chip," so I became Daddy's Lil' Cookie.

My daddy was the comic of the family, the glue that kept us together…until the glue loss its stickiness. Daddy, with his jovial characteristics, would capture our attention and kept us laughing, as he cracked jokes and played with us. He loved tickling us, and we loved his tickling.

I am reminded of a time when Gilbert and I were playing with Daddy. Daddy was tickling us, and we were laughing, laughing, laughing, and as we played, Gilbert was laughing so hard, he went into an asthma attack. He could not catch his breath for laughing. It was not funny, but it sure was comical. He could not inhale his medication because he could not stop laughing. Eventually, he settled down, but we then started cracking up at him for going into an attack. We could not stop laughing!

Daddy was so nervous and concerned. One day, Daddy and I were talking about that episode, and he told me he was so scared. He said when that happened, he felt helpless. Momma was the one who cared for Gilbert. After that, Daddy was very cautious when we played, and he learned how to care for Gilbert if he should go into an attack again on Daddy's watch. Daddy did not spare the rod, but he certainly did spoil *this* child.

Daddy was a kind person. He would give anyone the shirt off his back, but if someone made him mad, Daddy turned into an unrecognizable "violent stranger."

Chapter Two

Drugs and Daddy

When my dad was addicted to heroin and cocaine, I watched as he snorted, shot-up, and smoked drugs until he would nod out. He also smoked crack cocaine, got spooked and paranoid; then, he would start [iii]"tweaking," and that would go on for hours at a time. When he came to or down from his high, his first stop was the refrigerator. He raided the refrigerator of its bologna and watermelon; then, the cycle repeated itself. Daddy was a functional addict, until he was not. He worked for Saab Automotive, and every year, Saab gave me his new set of car keys. Daddy was no longer able to drive due to a Cocaine Induced Stroke, which left him handicapped and no longer able to drive. I was his caretaker and used his car to assist him in making sure he met his obligations. I had a Fiat, but Daddy did not like my car, so I drove his.

Years prior to his death Dad suffered the cocaine-induced stroke, and even after the stroke, I watched as Daddy mixed heroin and cocaine, melted it down, and shot-up. He called it a "Speedball." As a child, I got an old school butt whipping for picking up Daddy's needle. I was a little thing, and I did not know anything about a "hot" needle. A hot needle is a used needle that could possibly be infected with blood-borne disease(s). But, *Daddy had it, so it must have been alright,* was my thinking. I have always been an inquisitive person, and I was constantly touching, looking, or asking questions about something to better understand.

Nevertheless, after shooting-up, Daddy would start nodding and make me leave the room. I do not think he realized I was there until I tried to get a closer look as he nodded. Then, there were the times when Daddy hit Momz, and afterwards, he would lock himself in the bathroom and shoot-up.

I learned at a young age that drugs were a means of escape, to run from consequences and responsibility. My mottos were "upset-get high," "mad-get high," "happy-get high," "confused-get high," and "tired-get high." If you do not know what to do…just "get high" and "nothing to do, go ahead…get high." That was this young girl's mindset and perspective! Throughout most of my life, drugs, alcohol, and fast money were the center of my focus. My views on life were warped.

When I was introduced to the 12-Step Process of Alcoholics Anonymous and experienced the discipline and hope it gave to overcome my addictive personality, I encouraged my daddy to join a group in his area. I found an AA fellowship in San Pedro and Long Beach and took Daddy to them a few times. He celebrated my five-year sobriety birthday with me at U.S.P. and the 185 in Altadena. In 1997, Daddy gave me both cakes, and I shared with him how the fellowship helped me and gave me a new perspective on life. Daddy also saw the changes that occurred in my life, all for my betterment and continued to take place in my new life of "deliverance," but Daddy's response was, "I've done drugs as long as I can remember, and Imma die being who I am and doing what I do." Daddy rejected the fellowship, and just as night turns into day, he died a drug-related death.

I told you my daddy is deceased, but did I tell you he was murdered? I do not know the full details of his homicide and probably never will, but it was confirmed to be a drug deal gone badly. As Daddy's emergency contact, I was called to identify his body. What I saw burned its image into my very soul. Daddy was wedged between the wall and his bed, and blood was everywhere. Daddy was stuck in that position with his throat cut from ear to ear, and bugs were running in and out of his wounds.

When I received the call, I was working at Union Rescue Mission (URM) as an intake clerk, in the Women's Contact Office, and as one of the ministry chaplains and counselors. I was in the middle of chapel when my supervisor, Marty, who knew of the situation, called me from the podium. Marty informed me there was an important call I *had* to take from the San Pedro Police Department. Upon learning my dad was dead, I zoned out. It was me and my Lil' Peeps again, but it was God who carried me. I cannot tell you how I got from downtown Los Angeles to San Pedro, California. God was truly in control, and I made it in record time. I believed He transported me supernaturally because I do not remember driving.

While being interviewed by the police, I got a glimpse of the coroner's report, and it read *"Homicide."* While at the scene of his murder, I asked the officers, "What's going in the report and how are they listing Dad's death?" The response was, "Drug-related homicide: Drug deal gone badly." A case was opened and an investigation ensued; however, there are no answers to this date as to what prompted the horrific murder of a handicapped, elderly man. However, one thing I do know is Daddy's death was the outcome and the conclusion of him living a life of addiction.

I told you when Daddy got mad he turned into a "violent stranger." He had a fatal violent streak in him. When Daddy got mad, he was uncontrollable, especially if the altercation became physical. I had seen Daddy at his worse and witnessed him fighting to the bitter end. As a child, I was so hurt and troubled from seeing my daddy fighting. "Don't hit my Daddy," I cried, as I attacked the person Daddy was fighting. Momma came and grabbed me, picking me up off the floor from where I had been pushed to the ground. The fight then spiraled into an all-out battle; it was horrifying!

Daddy went to prison around 1958. I was five years old, but it seems like only yesterday. Daddy did time for burglary and shortly thereafter went to jail for a little over seven years because of his infidelity with my mother's first cousin, Peggy. He was charged with Breaking and Entering, Theft, and Attempted Rape, when all along cousin and Dad had been sleeping together for years. She even took a coat hanger to my dad's unborn child, conceived in the sorted affair. However, instead of telling the truth, she lied to protect herself.

Her boyfriend Johnson, came home early that day in November and found Cousin Peggy naked in the middle of the day. He questioned, "Why?" He was already suspicious of her, and Peggy did not have a valid reason why she was naked in the middle of the day, so Johnson commenced to searching the house. He found my daddy hiding in the closet. They fought, and Daddy jumped out of their bedroom window. *Well, you get the picture!*

Daddy ran straight home. However, he ended up doing time for Peggy's false allegations. Sometime later, around November or early December, Daddy was released and came home. My next memory picks up on Christmas Eve 1958, and there were no Christmas tree, Christmas dinner cooking, or gifts. Momma told us, "This is going to be a poor Christmas, but when I am able, I am going to make it up to you." Gilbert and I went to bed on Christmas Eve of 1958 very sad, but on Christmas day the first thing we noticed was the succulent aroma of Christmas dinner in the oven. We ran to the living room, and there was a tree and presents galore. There were so many presents; the living was full of gifts and Christmas cheer.

We started opening our gifts when there was a knock at the door. It was the Los Angeles Police Department. They handcuffed Daddy and took our gifts from under the tree, knocking the tree and its decorations over, taking Daddy, gifts and all. My brother and I were distraught. We were five and six. My brother Gilbert and I attacked one of the police officers. Thank God, they did not take my brother. I later learned Daddy had stolen our gifts from Douglas, Papa's (the owner) of the store, and Papa had Daddy arrested and our gifts confiscated.

A couple of times, we visited Daddy at Chino Men's Institute and were told and made to believe Daddy was in the hospital. Momma said I started reading at the age of five and not once did I see "hospital" in the name of Chino Men's Institute. A little over seven years later, at the ages of twelve and thirteen, we saw our daddy again. What a blessing.

Nevertheless, as we continued to venture through life with our mother, she began to date. Momma had divorced Dad while he was in prison, and we moved, taking us away from Grandma. I remember us living somewhere off Pico or Olympic Boulevard, where there was a pool hall on the corner. Momz introduced us to a man named Hillard Williams. She said he was her fiancé. To say the least, life for my brother and I took a turn for the worst.

Big Momma, Uncle Rev. and our First Cousins, "The Rollins"

Let me introduce my grandmother (Big Momma), uncle and his boys, my first cousins. Big Momma is Momz and Uncle Rev's mother. When we moved to 41st and Hooper, Big Momma lived in the front house, what I called the Sitting Room. She sat at the front window where she placed a table and three chairs. There she sat all day long, looking out that front window. There was an alley outside our gates and a court across the alley where Patsy Mae lived. Patsy Mae was Big Momma's bestie, and they would sit at that window regulating the neighborhood. Across Hooper Avenue was the neighborhood store where she had Harry, my cousin, and me cash her checks.

Big Momma was no joke. She chewed tobacco (snuff), smoked a pipe and, periodically, a cigar. She drank too. As she sat at that window, she had all the children believe she was drinking coffee. But one day, I asked Big Momma for a drink of her coffee. She said no; but I sneaked a drink and much to my surprise, it was not coffee. It was Whisky. She sipped on her Whisky all day long, and please, do not mess with Big Momma's Precious (her dog), or one of her babies, and we all were her babies. Daily, Big Momma and Patsy Mae sat at the table regulating, by yelling out the door, "You better stop that," or "Get in here, child." We used to have large family dinners, Big Momma cooked every holiday, and the family would gather. We had a good time, for the most part.

When we were children, all of us lived together. There was Uncle Rev., who had four boys: Leo, James, Harry, and Sam. Harry, Sam, and I were as close as brothers and a sister can be. We had so much fun together. Big Momma taught Harry and me how to cook, and she primarily took care of us while our parents worked. She took over because our mother and Uncle Rev. worked long hours, and my daddy was in prison.

During that time, the church was always open, from morning to about eight or nine o'clock every day. The people would come in to pray or sit and talk with my grandmother or uncle, and we were responsible to monitor and work with (play with) the neighborhood children, and the parking lot became the neighborhood play yard. We had a tetherball and an area designated for skating. We played handball, socking the ball against the church building. Everyone in the neighborhood knew us.

I was the only girl raised with Rev.'s four boys and my brother Gilbert. The five boys and I were inseparable. I was loved, spoiled, and protected by them and Uncle Rev. too. But, I was also a confused, battered, abused, and angry child. As I was exposed to and learned about God the Father, God the Son, and God the Holy Ghost, I felt inner warmth, love, and a sense of belonging, and on Easter Sunday morning around 1960, I met Him for myself.

Starting at Lent, every Easter holiday season, the church had some type of activity leading up to Resurrection Sunday, and on Resurrection Sunday, there was always a program. So, the Easter of 1960 was coming up, and the children were issued their Easter poems to learn and recite. I was seven and loved to sing. Uncle Rev. and Sister Ruben taught me to sing "The Old Rugged Cross." On that Easter Sunday morning, while the other children recited poems, I sang my first solo. I was so scared to the extent I started crying. Grandma said as I was singing when I begin to weep; then, I started crying like a baby, but I made it to the end of my song, glory be to God. Today, I understand what I experienced, as I sang for and to Jesus. The Spirit filled my soul, and my heart was overjoyed. Jesus baptized me with His Holy Spirit. I say that because I remember my brothers and I had our secret language, and the language I spoke then is the language I often hear and speak when the Spirit speaks through us in unknown tongues.

I was so excited when Uncle Rev. and Sis Ruben taught me to sing "The Old Rugged Cross." Singing is a passion that I have, and when I sing before God's people, it is a privilege and a blessing to be able to express my love, adoration, and appreciation unto Christ before the masses. I have sung in children choirs, youth and adult choirs, and groups. I have sung in nightclubs, at concerts, and on television, with the Lightner's and other groups. I did a three-show gig that ran for a week in Las Vegas, at the Horse Shoe, and I was a member of the U.S.P. Recovery Gospel Group in 1992–1993, and as a member, I was blessed to sing with Gladys Knight, but the Pips were not there. We were her opening act in Vegas, and she loved us and our thirst for music. Unfortunately, shortly thereafter, Frankie Harris, our leader, passed. When he died, so did the group. However, as a gospel soloist, I sing every opportunity I get, and every first Friday of the month, I am at Los Angeles Mission singing for the Lord and rightly dividing the Word of Truth to the homeless and disenfranchised.

I am a gospel soloist, and I love to sing Oldies but Goodies, Blues, and Jazz also. Just about every opportunity I get to sing, I will. However, I will never forget that first solo. I have often prayed to experience that feeling once again. That was when I consciously received Jesus Christ as my personal Lord and Savior. That is when I began to understand His presence in my life, and I started to recognize Him as that innate sense of love and belonging I felt as a child. I believe that was the day I first believed.

I did not know or understand I was traveling my Christian journey, and Jesus utilized me to be a living witness to the world, saying yes God is real. My life is proof positive that we will falter along the way, but God is still on the throne, and [iii]His grace is sufficient. He walked before me every step of the way, and I went to some horrid places; however, the Lord commenced to prepare me for what was ahead. My commission had been given, and I was deployed by God Himself to live this life I have lived and to tell you my story. His preparation for this present time was, as the songwriter wrote, [iv]"*A charge (call) to keep I have, a God to glorify.*" I know that now! But, I still had to yet learn some harsh life lessons, and as a child, the lessons I learned followed me like a shadow.

Second Cousins

Now, let me introduce you to my second cousins, the Clarks. My brother, first cousins, and I were close with the Clarks. Peggy was our mother's first cousin, and the one who had the affair with my daddy. Our second cousins were Larry, Richard, Glen, Donald, Bobbie, Deborah, and Brenda. Our grandmothers were sisters, and we usually had the card games at their home. Their house was big, and when the adults did their thing, we were in the back doing ours.

One evening, there was the Saturday night card game and Dominos as usual, and all the children were in the back. The older kids were getting high upstairs. Deborah brought me a drink, telling me it was spiked punch. We always drank spiked punch, so I did not give it a second thought. Well, that time I got smashed. I later found out that Deborah and a guy I did not know, put eye drops in an already spiked drink; I had been drugged. I vaguely recall, but that night, Momz was slapping folks around.

Momma told me I had been set up to be raped, but Momma caught the guy and put a hurtin' on him. All hell broke loose at Cousin Peggy's that night, and after that, everything started to unfold. I do not recall going on summer vacations with the Clarks after that incident and after that, at holiday dinners, Peggy and Momz always got into it.

One time, they got into an all-out brawl. That was the first time I saw my grandmother get angry enough to fight. Big Momma would take her cane and knock you the hell out! She had a method with her cane where she would trip you, and you would fall flat on your face. She would act so concerned, although tripping you was her intent all along. She would pat you on the back, while asking, "Baby, you okay?" She was so funny. When Big Momma chewed snuff, she could spit her tobacco juice clear across the room, and it landed in her spit can. I miss that ole' lady.

I have introduced the key characters of my early life's existence and experiences along with brief family interactions and other encounters. As a child, I lived a life of dependency, dependent on the elders. As I grew, the incidences I have shared molded me into well into adulthood. Those experiences wounded my personality, mentality, spirituality, emotionally and overall well-being. I grew up being someone shaped by abuse, molestation, anger, drugs, hurt, and pain. I entered adulthood with major trust issues, explosive untreated anger, and as a victim of abuse of multiple degrees, and the abuse overlapped, resurfacing in my personal relationships, on and off the job, and my marriage.

It has taken a long time for me to get to the point of acceptance. I had to accept what transpired to me as a child, and although I did not understand why I was stripped of my innocence, but I knew I had to grow past memories of the thief and offence. The agony and blatant acts of abuse impacted my life in a dangerous and negative fashion, I was dying, but I had to find common ground. I had to find solid ground and I needed to heal. I was paralyzed and unable to think straight and function maturely as an adult. I was dysfunctional in my daily affairs and failed to flourish as an adult; because of my past, it was problematic for me to move forward until I learned to forgive.

Anger and hatred invaded my mind, heart, soul, and spirit. My emotions were cold and callus, but one day, I cried unto the Lord and ᵛHe heard my cry and pitied every groan. I have crossed-over the junction of hatred, anger and discontentment to the shores of forgiveness with peace. Still, I operated in a foul state of mind much of my life, but now, I have healed emotionally, and my mental health is of the Lord's, as I keep my mind stayed on Him and seek things above. Daily, I pursue the Lord with all I have and all I have to give.

I seek Jesus early in the morning, I need His Holy Ghost power to face daily agitations and challenges. I look to Him moment by moment for peace, love and under-standing because that's all I have is "this very moment," which is now past and gone, never to return unto me again. I have peace, in Him. *"Peace I leave with you, My peace I give you…"* (John 14:27 KJV). He said, "I leave," because He was preparing the people for His ascension. You know Jesus is coming back soon, folks.

In our world, today and according to Revelation 12:7-12, Satan has but a short time to reign and his number is about up. We are in the 2000th year and the 17th hour of Christ's return. We must watch, Jesus is on His way back Saints!

Rev. 3:3 reminds us to, *"Remember therefore how thou hast…heard…hold fast and repent. …thou shalt not watch, I will come on thee as a thief, …I will come upon thee."* The Saints of old tell us: "Be diligent. Don't let the Lord catch you with your work undone!"

This is a Pomegranate Tree

 This is a Pomegranate

Chapter Three

Now you have an idea of my early childhood experiences and what it was like for me. At this point in my story, we moved from a garage apartment into our first home. It was a big house off Central Avenue on 42nd Place.

I recall we had a humongous backyard where there was a pomegranate bush and a peach tree we climbed. Also, there was a garage where Uncle Rev. lived and an old shack in the back with a chicken coup. That is where the boys, neighborhood kids, and I hung out most of the time. We would watch Big Momma as she would catch a chicken and wring its neck. That chicken would run in circles with its head dangling, hanging, and flopping around until it died. Then, there were times Big Momma took a small axe and chopped the head off. However, the chicken still ran in circles, but it died faster. We were taught to pluck its feathers and gut it. I hated that part!

To the east of us was an apartment building with at least six to eight units, and every unit had a child, or two, or three, and we all knew each other. I told you the boys were older than I was and smoked lots of marijuana. Well, on a typical day, after school, we would have a snack, do homework, and play outside. However, the boys smoked joints, ate lots of candy and junk food, played, and had fun. So, at the age of nine, I sneaked into our cousin's room, took a joint, and smoked it. That was just the beginning! I liked the way it made me feel. I felt happy, and everything was funny. I had not laughed like that in a long time, and I wanted to continue to laugh, so I continued to sneak joints.

Big Momma's bedroom was off the kitchen, which was enormous to me, and the bathroom connected our room to hers. Momz and Dad slept on the sofa bed in the living room. The boys and I slept in the room off the service porch, where there was a washbasin with hot and cold running water and a toilet. There were four beds lined up side by side where Sam, Harry, Gilbert and James slept; my bed was on the other side of the room by the bathroom that connects to Big Momma's room.

There was an additional small room where Leo had a bed and dresser. He had his own space. He was the oldest, and he was tall too, 6'7". When it was lights out, I hid under my blanket. The boys always scared me, by poking me and making shadow images and scary sounds. Those are fond memories.

I love to reminiscence on the family outings and holiday dinners. Our family had many house parties, many picnics, dinners, and of course, the weekend card games. We celebrated everything, and I was raised and taught family unity and *"to do unto others as you'd have others do unto you,"* and that is the Golden Rule. I was taught *"right is right, and right don't wrong nobody,"* and that was Momma's rule. But the way family treated me, except for my daddy and uncle, was not what I was being taught. I was taught to *"tell the truth no matter what,"* and *"the truth can get you into trouble, but it will get you out of trouble also."* This is another adage from Momz. She taught me to tell the truth no matter how much it hurts. But when I did that…hell yeah it hurt. My butt was torn up several times a day for some things I did, but mostly for what I did not do! But that hurt was not of the flesh. My feelings, heart, and my spirit were hurt and eventually terminally wounded and broken by family, the ones I loved the most and trusted!

At some point, we moved to Hooper Avenue, across the street from Jefferson High School, which was up the street and around the corner from the other house. We lived at 4113 and 4113½ S. Hooper Ave. We were right next door to a hole-in-the-wall hamburger stand, and I loved their chili cheese burgers.

They were delicious! That house was the first property my grandmother purchased.

Uncle Rev. and the boys moved to their first home on Harvard Blvd. off Adams. We started going over there on weekends; we had fun! One day, Harry and I were playing, and I jumped onto Harry's back, and their dog bit me on the ankle. I beat the mess out of that dog as I sat there bleeding. Off to General Hospital we went, and I had to get a rabies and tetanus shot. Nevertheless, at the end of the day, that dog and I became the best of friends. He never bit me again either!

I remember being a child and walking the boys to school with Big Momma. The boys always walked in front, and I walked hand in hand with Big Momma behind them. As we walked, if a Caucasian was seen walking on the sidewalk ahead of or behind us, Grandmother would make us cross the street. If there was a Caucasian on that side, she directed us to walk in the street single file. It was clandestine oppression, much as it is today. Later, I started kindergarten and by then, the boys walked to school by themselves.

The neighbors knew all of us, and eventually, I was allowed to walk to school with the boys. You know that saying, "It takes a village to raise a child"? We were members of the 41st Street village; the neighbors actively participated in caring for the neighborhood children, and my kindergarten teacher knew my family very well. She was also aware of my family's disposition towards me and how I was horribly treated. The unfairness was evident in how I was treated opposed to the boys. I could not figure out what was wrong with me. I grew up believing I was an outcast, and as I researched my family's history for this book, it was recently revealed that I wasn't the only one being violated, stripped of their innocence, and tossed out like refuse.

We went to Wadsworth Elementary School in the 60s. Every day, we started school with prayer first, followed by the Pledge of Allegiance. The method of discipline was much different than it is now. The principals were allowed to swat the students with a paddle, and our principal's paddle had holes in it. So, when a student was swatted, his/her butt would be sucked into those holes. "OUCH!" that hurt! The paddle and my butt knew each other far too well. Soon, Momma moved us, and we transferred to Virginia Road Elementary School. There were fond memories, especially the culmination. That was a good period of time when the molestation stopped, *until* my mother's boyfriend moved in with us!

I was a bright and intelligent child and earned good grades, *until I didn't*. In high school, I played the trumpet in the marching band and enjoyed cheerleading. I did that, *until I didn't*. Because of times past, I learned to hide my feelings of inferiority, guilt, and deprivation. I grew up with an inferiority complex, feelings of being less than. I felt I was nothing, and shame weighed me down. I was a wounded soul, and I never finished anything. I was not taught perseverance or commitment. I was never taught to see things to the end. I was never taught to finish what I started. I was told to finish, but I was never shown, encouraged, or empowered. I just did not know how! I always quit- right before the victory or breakthrough.

Every day and every night, my poor wounded heart cried, as the roars of the oppressor yelled loudly and boisterously over my head, drowning out my dreams and instilling a deep resentment for the insurrection. I was hurt, angry, and malicious! I learned to fight and fight wickedly, as I tried to hurt my opponent, failing to see and understand it was a spiritual battle and not a physical one.

Anger and fierceness manifested around thirteen or fourteen years of age. It was like an overloaded cistern that blew its whistle. I felt no one loved me, and I did not care! I was not alone although I was haunted with feelings of alienation, hate, abuse, and unworthiness. I felt alone; however, there was something innate that assured me I would be alright. Upon culminating from Virginia Road, I was sent to Foshey Junior High School where I was kicked out for ditching and fighting. I was sent straight to John Adams Junior High where Aunt Eula, Uncle Rev.'s second wife was the vice principle.

Because of close supervision, I finished at John Adams Junior High, as a straight 'A' student and transferred to Los Angeles High School (LAHS). Things were beginning to look up and promising; I was excited! Nevertheless, the anger was untreated. I often wondered if my mother knew there was help for me, to aid me in learning to control my temperament or if therapy was affordable for us.

Blacks were still being treated as inferior, and I was constantly picked on and bullied. On the flip side of all that anger, I was timid. Everything I encountered caused me to be withdrawn and spiteful. When triggered, I would take off on a person and attack. I would blackout, and the only conscious thought I would have was that of drawing blood from the antagonist. I was later diagnosed with blackout rages and was reported to the sheriff as having blackout rages with homicidal tendencies. The doctor had to submit a report to the Los Angeles Sheriffs, stipulating I threatened to wait for Jill Conrad in the parking lot and follow her with the intent of bringing bodily harm upon her. I worked at High Desert Hospital as an Los Angeles County Employee Intermediate Typist Administrator/Time Keeper Level 3, and Jill was my supervisor.

Jill insulted and degraded me verbally with racial remarks and slurs that she laughed at because she thought it was funny. Jill also circulated printed racial jokes, slurs, and remarks and had the audacity to give me a copy of them. I felt degraded by her jokes and comments, and she did that in the presence of my co-workers. Several joined Jill in laughing, thinking it was funny, but there was not anything funny about that. I was insulted!

As time went on, things changed, and Blacks and Whites learned to co-exist. Blacks and Whites could walk on the same block, go to school together, and go to the same markets. Racial tensions soon quieted, for a while. When we rode the bus, there were Whites on our buses, and we saw them downtown. In the beginning, it was uncomfortable, and I felt scared to be close to a white person. That fear and discomfort soon dissipated when I started going to school with them.

I have fond memories of those bus rides with Big Momma and the weekend gatherings. At those gatherings, I learned to play Bid Whist, Gin Rummy, Spades, Poker, and Seven Card Stud. Also, at those card games, we met lots of uncles and male cousins, which I recently found out were not kin at all. During that era, when family brought an unfamiliar face around, out of respect, they were introduced as a cousin or uncle so-n-so. During that era, our parents instilled respect, and we had to "put a handle" on it. In other words, we had to address an adult with Mr., Mrs., Sir, Madam, Uncle, or Cousin. Well, you catch the drift. I also remember going to South Park with Daddy. He played dominoes, as my brother and I roamed the park and surrounding neighborhoods. South Park is where Daddy taught me to play dominoes (bones) as I sat on his lap. He taught me to count and recognize which "bone" had been played.

Growing up in Los Angeles in the 60's was so much different than it is today. L.A. has not always been congested, busy, and developed as it is today. I was around ten, and I remember walking to the haunted house on Sunset and Vine with the boys. It took us no time to get there. We would hang out in Hollywood and make it back home before dinner. Then, we had flat land to walk across. In addition, we skated to the Coliseum, skating there all day long, then skated back home just in time for "Street Lights No Punches," a game we used to play as the street lights came on. These are fond memories, where the boys and I had fun, fun, and more fun. We also could be a terror, and a terror we were.

As a young girl, I did not have female friends. The boys were all I really knew, and that was my norm. The only girls I had constant contact with were my second cousins: Deborah and Brenda, with whom we took vacations. The neighborhood girls did not like me because I hung with the boys and their friends hung with us. A girl may have liked one of the boys or their friend and asked me to hook them up. I would introduce them, and that was it. However, if the boy did not respond to the girl, I became the enemy.

In the eyes of the boys' friends, I was "Cookie," their little sister. Some girls pretended they wanted to be my friend and hang with me. That was their plot to get closer to a boy they liked. I did not care one way or the other. They could hang, but all they wanted to do was sit around, snack, talk (gossip), flirt, and giggle. That was not me. I liked to be in the mix. So, I rode the bikes, climbed the trees, and skated with the boys. The girls felt I deserted them, but I would tell them, "Go get your bike, skates, and let's roll." They did not, so I rode with the boys or solo.

When the girls were rejected or dumped, they always turned on me, and as we got older, the bad talk started; I was called a hoe, slut, and a loose girl. That made me angry and not too friendly. I stayed in fights. The harbored anger ate at me to the point I felt everyone had it out for me. Today, they would call it paranoid. I became even more hostile, rude, and suspicious towards everyone.

Chapter Four
Summertime in Oakland
[vi]*Summertime, and the Living is Easy* "NOT!"...

There is one thing I must let you know: My family loves me, but during that era, they were crazy sick. When I say sick, they were certifiably S I C K! By today's standards, there would be diagnoses of Bi-Polar, Schizophrenia, Psychosis, Paranoid Schizophrenia, Psychosis with Homicidal/Suicidal Tendencies and Ideations, and other diagnosis you can find listed in the [vii]DSM-5, (Diagnostic and Statistical Manual of Mental Disorders Fifth Edition).

In most families, there is a "black sheep," and all my life, I filled that position in my family. I noticed I was treated differently, and many times, my feelings were hurt. There was always a reason why my brother consumed Momma's love, time, and attention. I understood he was sickly with childhood asthma, as I watched Momma care for him. Afterwards, she would be so drained; all she could do was rest. His attacks were serious, and Mother always told me I was her strong little girl and I was a good child. Folks, FYI-strong people have moments, and they are subject to weakness, too! They are prone to fragility and strong people need encouragement, empowerment and comfort too; they need time out to be comforted and cared for also.

Nonetheless, recognizing the differentiation in treatment, I began to mimic the boys and took on their behaviors and attitudes. I enjoyed climbing trees and racing on Schwinn Sting Ray bicycles with lawn mower engines mounted on them. My God, those were fun times. We had ourselves a ball. I also remember the boys taught me as we were walking if I saw an unattended bike to jump on it and take off. After getting a few, we would go on a scavenger hunt for lawn mower engines. After acquiring enough, the boys would mount the engines on the bikes, creating a moped-like cycle, and we would ride them all over L.A.

The one thing that always happened once caught, we would, of course, get in a lot of trouble. But then again, I stayed in trouble. I was blamed for just about everything. For the most part, only Sam and Harry would stand up for me, unless it was something serious, then Gilbert would. And boy, don't let somebody else lie on or hit me. The boys would beat the person senseless. After beating the person, they would turn to the crowd and invite others to jump in and get whipped. But at home, I got blamed for everything, and for me, that was confusing, and it hurt!

I think around that time Uncle Rev. and Eula P. moved to Harbor City, and we started going to Harbor City on weekends and holidays. Harbor City at that time was untouched; there were lots of marsh and swamp-like terrain. The boys and I were exploring the terrain when I fell on a broken bottle. The marsh had covered the broken glass, and my hand was badly cut. Off to Harbor General I went, to get stitched up. We all were grounded, and everyone blamed me, but I was following the boys. I did not know we were not to be in that area.

I must say, the boys and I had nothing but fun out there; our only problem was Aunt Eula. She had no children, could not have children, and did not want any children. To say the least, she was shell shocked to then have five boys and a girl to contend with and heaven help when it was all thirteen of us. We ran her crazy and always denied our behavior to Uncle Rev. Of course, he believed us (for a minute that is).

Like clockwork, during the summer, all the children went to Oakland, California. It was me, his five boys, and our second cousins, totaling thirteen: ten boys and three girls. Every summer, we rode the Amtrak Train or Greyhound Bus to Aunt Gladys and Uncle Frank's; the fun we had during those outings were euphoric, but painful too.

Aunt Gladys was our grandma's baby sister. Aunt Gladys did not have children, and she was retired. Auntie smoked more marijuana than the boys and Puff the Magic Dragon combined! Uncle Frank was an engineer with Southern Pacific Railways and transported cargo. On our vacations, we often went to work with him and rode in one of the empty cars. We rode trains and trolley cars like crazy and played up and down Fishermen's Wharf for hours. Oh, my God, the joy, fun, and freedom I felt as we rode those cars, played on the wharf, and went to church with Aunt Gladys remains with me to this very day. It is one of those childhood memories that reminds me of innocence and adventure, **then,** pain and abuse. Wow, there is always a **"then"**!

Even at Auntie's house in Oakland, I was treated differently. My cousins would lie on me. And my brother went along with them. I felt hopeless. Why didn't my brother step up? One morning, all the kids were hungry. Most of us ate cereal, but for some reason my cousin Richard cooked a pot of Cream of Wheat, which was my favorite.

Richard got in trouble for cooking the Cream of Wheat. To vindicate himself, he told Auntie I asked him to cook it. That was a lie, and everyone knew it, but no one stood up for me. They all sided with Richard and said I asked him to cook it. Auntie made me eat the whole pot of Cream of Wheat with no butter, sugar or cream. I was forced to eat until I became so full

I felt sick. I told Auntie I could not eat anymore, so she sat over me with the belt and force-fed me. I tried to eat more but threw up. Auntie beat me and made me eat the vomitus. I do not remember anything else about that incident after I knelt over the puke. I retreated to my Lil' Peoples Land!

Afterwards, everyone felt bad and tried to comfort me, but there was no comfort for me when all they had to do was speak up but did not. Once we were home from vacation, Momma was told what happened. I got in trouble all over again. Still no one spoke up. I had to forgive my siblings and cousins for that incident and so much more. I do not understand and do not have an answer, but I held that close to my heart for a long time. Today, I purpose to hold onto the good times and let go of the bad, as I learn to survive and thrive. I had a yearning to live and be left alone!

Chapter Five

Between being victimized and becoming an unwed teen mom, I remember my appearance and hair being admired by folks. Sometimes, I felt as though I was being "showcased." As previously stated, I was introduced to men who were presented as an uncle or cousin. Strangers were allowed to stroke my hair and talk about how pretty I was, and that was a constant, causing me to feel uncomfortable. If I would say something about being uncomfortable, I would be chastised, scolded and told I ought to be grateful for the beauty I was born with. But I never felt beautiful. As those acts took place, I would look to see who would be my uncle or cousin for that evening and what they were going to do to me, and those were just a few of my fears.

When going with Momz to weekend card games or the club, there would come a time when all the children were sent out of the room, sometimes one by one. Nevertheless, I would find myself alone, wondering why I was not sent out. Soon, after realizing I was alone, that so-called uncle or cousin would come in to see about me and proceed to touch and grope me.

I had been violated since the tender age of nine, and that went on for years. The molestation got worse and became more frequent. I was accused of enticing men and was told I needed to "cease my behavior." I did not know what entice meant, but to say the least, I eventually stopped telling! There was a saying of old that goes something like this, "If she's eight, it's too late, but nine is prime. Get it, and take your time." I am sure you understand what that means, and it was not nice.

For years, *the thief of my innocence* went disregarded and unavenged; no one believed me, except my brother Gilbert. But when I told my daddy, he went ballistic. I got whipped and punished for starting trouble. I had no intention to start trouble. My daddy asked me questions, and I answered him. Why Momma whipped me, heaven only knows. But then again, my daddy had the tendency to get real ignorant when it came down to me, and because of the chain of events that followed, my emotions became even more disarrayed. I was angry. I became hostile, rude, and confrontational. Daddy told me I was not wrong for being upset and had the right to be angry, but I was so vile and such an unlovable creature, disrespectful, unfriendly, and trifling that Daddy became upset with me, and that hurt more than any butt whipping Momma could have given me. Nevertheless, Daddy explained the molestation and abuse were not mine to own, but he held me accountable for my actions and behaviors. He said I was being violated and what was happening was wrong, and he would take care of it, but he continued to chastise me nonetheless, for being difficult and disrespectable to Momma, but most of all, for not coming to him sooner.

Finally, I was big enough to resist and defend myself. Daddy told me the next time someone tried to touch me to hurt him. He taught me where to kick and what to grab, and that is just what I did. I kicked Uncle so-n-so very hard between the legs that his ball bearings were coming out of his nose and his stick shift no longer operated. Momma and I talked about it, cried, and tried to let it go, but I yet harbored anger, resentment, and bitterness and I did not know how to act or what to do with these ill-will feelings. I would explode at the slightest indication, and I was brutal Daddy said. Momma told me that was around the time I started sneaking around communicating with my dad, but she accused me of telling him her business and she was right. I told my Daddy everything, good, bad and ugly.

Daddy was then actively involved in my life, and that put a greater strain on me and Mother's relationship. Momz did not know I stayed in contact with Daddy at first, and we constantly argued. It became common, and by then, I had a deep resentment towards her and became even more rebellious. I was then tagged as an out-of-control teen by the Los Angeles Unified School District and sent to Betsy Ross High School. I was in the tenth grade. Betsy Ross was run by the Los Angeles County Sheriffs and I completed the tenth grade there, and during that time frame, it was my second semester during the first quarter of the eleventh grade that I became pregnant! The school placed me in their educational program for pregnant teens. In that program, I had to call in at eight o'clock, and class started at 8:15am. I would call in, turn on the radio and television, do roll call, and be sleep by 8:20. That happened too often, so I was released from the program. I had no ambition; I was not taught how to manage my time. I was not pushed to get out the bed, go to the table, and do my school work. Also, I had no help with my daughter until I left home and married. Willie B. was my first husband and the father of my two youngest children and the stepfather for my eldest child, whom he loved as his own.

The abuse went from being victimized by friends of the family to my mother's boyfriends, except Al; he was the good one. One of Momma's boyfriends was Al Harper. He loved my momma, and he loved us. He was good to my brother and me; we liked him. Al babysat us until Momma made it in from work. When they broke up, we were sad for a long time.

Momma then started seeing Williams, and he violated me. I told you I was accused of leading him on. Nonetheless, one morning, my brother Gilbert saw I was upset and insisted I tell

43

him what happened. He pressured me and out it came. I blurted out what Hillard Williams did. I told you a little about Hillard in my mother's introduction. After telling Gilbert, it seemed as if he lost his mind because he jumped Williams. I was terrified! Momma tried breaking up the fight but could not. She began shouting at me, asking me what "I" did. I told her what happened. She then began making humiliating remarks as she put Williams out.

This is what transpired: I was about thirteen, and my bedroom was next to the bathroom where I was bathing. I finished my bath, wrapped myself in a towel, and put on my terrycloth robe. I tied the robe and went into my bedroom. My closet had a dressing room, and that is where I went, took off the robe, and commenced to drying and oiling my body when suddenly, my closet door flung opened. It was Williams. He walked in, grabbed me, and started doing what he did.

Honestly, I was constantly criticized and very little was constructive. I was scared to tell my mother because there was a previous incident when he had touched me inappropriately. I told, and I got in trouble. I was scolded and told to stop whatever it is I was doing! WHAT? I did not get that. What "I" was doing? Williams left, and we never saw him again. My mother believed my brother and then, she believed me, but it took my brother to tell her the same thing I had been telling her for some time. I felt forever cursed and remained *the accused.*

At that point, I was experimenting with and using drugs heavily. I have always loved music, and daily, I surrounded myself with Jazz, Gospel, Blues, Waterscapes, or Smooth Jazz. My brother and I used to sing together in choirs and groups. In the late 70s, Gilbert and I, along with our father, older brother Darryl, and my BFF's husband, formed a group called "T.L.C."

The Lord's Connection©. We were in demand in the South Bay and L.A. areas.

Wow! As I write, I can feel "ghost pains," the pain, the degradation, and shame of it all. Ghost pain is what an amputee experiences after having a limb removed; it feels like the limb is still there after surgery. I was very young, but I was taking Red Devils, LSD, Truanol, Black Mollies, Speed and Mini Bennies, or what we then called "Whites." I constantly retreated to Lil' Peoples land, running from the realities of my life. The inflicted damage took me to the dark places of gloom and doom, and literally, down death's corridor. But, I made it. God's grace and mercy covered me and protected me from all hurt, harm, and danger. I have been forgiven, and now, the life I have lived is the testimony I *MUST* give!

The manifestation of hostile behavior revealed itself like a tsunami during my junior year of high school. In the 60s and 70s, we went to high school in the tenth grade, and by then, I was fighting again. I became verbally hostile and disrespectful, with a vicious mentality for fighting. I was kicked out of Los Angeles High School and sent to Dorsey High; I was kicked out of there, for ditching and, you got it, fighting. I was then sent to Crenshaw High and from there to Fairfax High. At that time, Fairfax was predominately Caucasian, and I am black and was a Black Panther. I was a light-skinned black girl with long hair. Daily, I was teased and called an "Oreo."

The girls would come up behind me, pull my hair, crack jokes, and say cruel things to me. One day that happened, and I snapped. I grabbed the girl, threw her to the ground, and commenced to bash in her face. Three male teachers attempted to break up the fight, but I had the girl in my grips and was not letting go. As the teachers tugged and pulled, I squirmed my way to the railing and threw her over. Down a flight of cement steps, she went. I did not mean to hurt her, *but hurt I did!* Her arm was broken in three places. She suffered a dislocated collar bone and fractured wrist. Her leg was twisted in an awkward position, and she had to have physical therapy. She was banged up pretty badly. Although she admitted to instigating the fight, I was still kicked out of Fairfax due to the extreme exhibition of violent behavior. That is when I was sent to Betsy Ross High, the facility I mentioned earlier. It was a county-run educational facility controlled by the L.A. County Sheriff Dept., and they ran that facility with strict guidelines and expectations of its students. But, that school was the last stop (as a child) on the block. The next exit was adulthood!

Back then, there were no incentives or programs available to blacks. We were not encouraged or taught to seek higher education. However, Uncle Rev. was an advocate for higher education and instilled the importance of education in the boys and me. Education equals intelligence, intelligence equals power, and success is the power of intelligence unleashed. Uncle Rev. drilled into our minds that once a person attains education, no one can take it from him/her. I wanted to stay in school and learn. I tried. I tried to do all the right things, but it seemed like it was never enough.

While at Betsy Ross, I met Deborah Lusby, and we quickly became BFFs. Deborah and I started hanging together at school, and after school, I sometimes went home with her. We met each other's brother, and she fell for Gilbert, and I fell for Larry. Deborah and Gilbert are about the same age. I was fifteen, and Larry was twenty-one, but we were a perfect match. I think because of my history, I gravitated towards older men. Larry and I fell in love. We saw each other as often as possible. He was military. Larry asked Momz and Pops for my hand in marriage. He was denied and forbidden to ever see me again. That night, Gilbert and I hooked up with Deborah and Larry. We cooked up some [viii]*Vietnam Brew*, smoked a couple of joints, and were having a good time. Gilbert and Deborah went into one room, while Larry and I went into the other.

Larry and I discussed my mother's decision and decided to check into emancipation, and that was the night I conceived our daughter La'Shawn Lusby. Deborah was the first I told I was pregnant, and she was elated that she was going to be an auntie. But the very next day, she acted as if she did not know me. I found out her mother Elizabeth got wind I was pregnant, and Deborah accused me of lying. Deborah acted as if she knew nothing about Larry and me. She acted as if she was upset and furious. And me? I was so baffled!

Momz jammed me about my cycle, and although she already knew I was pregnant, she forced me to tell her about Larry and me. My mother was not very happy. She confronted Larry, his father, and his mother, Elizabeth. Things became heated between the mothers. Elizabeth was uppity and looked down on our family. To say the least, Deborah turned on me like a viper. At first, I thought she was acting that way in front of her mom, but the things that came out of Deborah's mouth was derogatory, hurtful, and detrimental. That really hurt. I had experienced difficulties bonding with females. They were envious, jealous, and treacherous. But, I valued our friendship. I thought Deborah and I had a meaningful bond, and I enjoyed having a female friend.

However, when all that happened, I was shattered within, and I made a promise to myself that I was going to hurt her just as badly as she hurt me, and I knew where to hit. I was young, vindictive, and trifling. I was without a conscious, for it had been seared. After a period of time, things changed, and we reconnected. Deborah and I began to associate again, but she never apologized or acknowledged La'Shawn as a Lusby. As time marched on, I cunningly separated Bobby from Deborah. That went on for a while, and her husband took good care of 'Shawn and me.

Then, I accidently, *on purpose,* let it slip that Bobby and I had it going on. Also, Deborah had started suspecting Bobby had stepped out on her, but I was the furthest from her mind, on her list of suspects. That was well after Larry's demise. After the affair came out, I did what I set out to do, hurt her just as badly as she hurt me. Deborah scornfully chose to deny my daughter La'Shawn as her niece and rejected my baby the right to know her family.

After Larry was killed *(or so I thought. His death certificate indicates suicide),* Deborah went on a campaign to publicize that she was disowning 'Shawn, and she is still bitter. Before Larry's death, Larry told his father, Poppa Lusby, that La'Shawn was his child, and Poppa Lusby accepted and loved her as his granddaughter. He tried telling Elizabeth and Deborah, but they continued their hateful rampage.

Time passed, and 'Shawn was about three years old. Deborah forbade Bobby to continue playing with T.L.C. as the drummer. One evening, we had rehearsal at Darryl's, in Long Beach. Everyone was present, except Bobby, who was late. As the timekeeper, upon his arrival, I inquired about him being late. He said Deborah forbade him to continue with T.L.C., but he came anyway, and all hell broke loose. Deborah came to rehearsal and went off on Bobby, but he was still there for the next rehearsal.

Chapter Six
True Love Interrupted… My Baby's Daddy

Again, I felt rejected, but not just me. I was hurting for my daughter, too. For years, her father's dad would call me over to Crenshaw High School where he was a mathematician, or he would stop by our place on 9th Avenue, just across from Crenshaw High, on his way home. He always blessed 'Shawn and me. He accepted my child and had a great bond with her. She called him Poppa or Pawpaw. He said he saw the likeness of his son in her. They became attached, and she loved seeing her grandfather. But, that ended after he retired. Although he continued to send funds, he was missed. The visits suddenly stopped, and 'Shawn began to ask for Pawpaw. His wife found out, and that was the end of all communication with Poppa Lusby.

I was bitter, bewildered, and experienced a flood of emotions, including resentment, antipathy, and rage that turned to hatred. I became vengeful; it was difficult enough that my first love and child's dad was dead. Then, having to deal with his trifling sister disgusted me. Today, Deborah has a beautiful niece, great nieces and great nephews, all offspring of her brother whom she does not know. One of my grandsons looks just like Larry. My heart goes out to Deborah; she is on her deathbed and continues to deny the truth. 'Shawn and I keep her in our prayers.

Let me tell you about my baby's daddy! Larry was military during the Vietnam War. The year we decided to defy family and friends and get married, he was killed. In the early 70s, I was fifteen, and he was twenty-two. He came home from his tour in Vietnam and asked my mother for my hand in marriage.

She refused him. Her reasoning was she did not want me to leave; we were going to move to Missouri. Although my love was interrupted by Momz' refusal, we were engaged anyway and not to long afterwards, we got pregnant with our daughter. Larry was around the majority of the pregnancy, but he had to report to base. So, he missed our baby's birth.

For the birth of our daughter, I thought my mother was there to be supportive. I was leery and untrusting, but I wanted and needed my mother's support. Her first response was for me to have an abortion, but I was too far along. So reluctantly, I accepted the help of my mother that I earnestly wanted, needed, and desired. I was scared, baffled, in pain, and about to have a baby. Although she appeared to be sincere in her efforts of being there for me, I soon suspected she was up to something. But what? Momz has a way of playing games; she will have you caught up in a trick bag in a cool minute. She was good at running game too, but I am my mother's daughter, and I was ready to fight for my baby.

I had La'Shawn in 1970. Back then, they gave you a Spinal Tap, and after delivering your baby, you had to lay flat on your back for twelve to twenty-four hours. Well, shortly after delivery, my mother and another woman came into my room, attempting to have me sign adoption papers for my mother to adopt my daughter. They came into my hospital room with paperwork, saying I needed to sign my baby's birth certificate. My father, early in life, taught me to read the fine print before signing my name to anything and to make sure I know what it is I am signing. That day, the relationship I had with my mother changed forever and not for the best. That was the first time I ever cursed my mother. Those papers were adoption papers.

Time marched on, and Larry and I were planning to elope and start our lives together with our baby, who was then around two years old. She was the sparkle in her father's eye. He was up for an honorable discharge, and we were excited, happy, and preparing to marry. Larry was hurt, sad, and upset because his mother and siblings were against me and denied his daughter. We decided to have a small intimate ceremony; Viva Las Vegas was our destination, to the Cupid Wedding Chapel. My mom turned vicious when she got wind we were going to marry, but regardless of what she or anyone else thought or said...*to hell with them, all of them*... as long as we had each other. That was our mindset.

I had a stepbrother Homer. He was a detective with the Los Angeles Police Department (LAPD), and my mother had him get Larry's background history. She told me Larry was married and already had two children. She began calling him a liar and a cheat, telling me what he was doing with me, he would do to me. Nevertheless, I do not know if she created the lie or if Homer trumped up a false report and presented it to her, but it was a lie—or so I thought.

During my extensive research for details and facts as I wrote my story, I learned he was in fact married. Still, whatever the report was I insisted it was falsified, and I rejected the report. I was young, dumb, and in love. Momma and I grew even further apart, and I stayed mad. Every night I went to bed with an attitude, and every morning, I woke up with insolence in my heart. Meanwhile, I remained disrespectful to my momma. I tried to get away from her, but she would not let me leave. She kept telling me to calm down. And that is all she wanted me to do was "calm down." But, I was angry and unruly. I think I smart mouthed Momma, yet whatever it is I did or said, Momz grabbed me. I turned, broke her grip, and acted as if I were going to do something.

My mother is barely five feet tall, and I am about 5'6." Well, that ole' woman grabbed me by the throat, dragged me through the living room, around the corner, through the hall, and to the bathroom where she literally tossed me into the bathtub and commenced to choke the living daylights out of this sista'. I was high and already emotionally and mentally phased out, and she then, she was trying to take me out. You know that cliché? You probably said it yourself; I know I have.

Momma was yelling, "I brought you into this world, and I'll take you out!" Thank God for my brother Gilbert who heard us and came to pull Momma off me. He got her off, but she still had my throat in her clutches, and my brother struggled to loosen her hands.

By then, I trusted only God and my fiancé, and my trust in God had diminished! I was a sixteen-year-old high school dropout and mother without a clue. I felt lost and bewildered, but I was resolute. With all that had happened, the hurt and tensions between my mother and me left me feeling drained and empty.

Daily hurt compounded upon hurt was my fate. The ones I loved and trusted became the crust of my agony. I needed justification/vindication for my daughter and me. Deborah was at the center of the confusion and commotion, so it was she I wanted, and I knew just where to hit to make her hurt. I *needed* her to feel the pain she inflicted on me, the pain I felt *but worse*. I wanted her to hurt, badly hurt! She was denying my daughter, speaking badly about me, and lying to her family about Larry and my relationship. That was another one of those moments when I felt impending doom. You know what is so ironic about that? As I write, expounding on my life experiences, I am reminded of the condition of my heart and…it was ugly.

I shake my head at the person I had become. I was not kind at all. Although I was professing to be a Christian, I operated in anger and hostility. I have learned forgiveness empowers a person to move on living in profuse delightfulness and joy in the Lord, free from the pangs of unforgiveness. 'Shawn hurts behind all of this, but she prays for Deborah. She cries for Deborah. Although she has forgiven Deborah, still 'Shawn continues to be horribly talked about and mistreated by her auntie Deborah. 'Shawn is my sentimental one, and she is so preciously emotional.

One day, Deborah coaxed me into a controversial discussion. I gave in and engaged in voicing my opinion. Soon we found ourselves at odds, which was nothing new. Quickly the conversation escalated into a shouting match and whatever was said and/or done, Deborah became unraveled and took it to another level. She was holding La'Shawn, and after cursing me, she held my baby away from her body as if she was a pile of dung. Deborah proceeded to tell my baby, "You ain't nothing but a yellow bastard with no daddy!" Then, she turned to shout at me, bellowing, "No one wants a yellow monkey and its mother like you." I will never forget her words. They cut just like a knife, and her true sentimentality resurfaced. I have no further recollection of what transpired afterwards I was outraged, and I phased out.

Forgiving

However, I must acknowledge, accept and admit the role I played in Deborah's bitterness. There is no excuse for the things I did against her and the pain I inflicted upon her. There is no excuse. It disquiets my spirit that what I did she will take to her grave. It disquiets my spirit I caused so much anguish to another human being. It disquiets my spirit because I was a stumbling block, a thorn in the side of another, causing her to live with the constant reminder of pain, disloyalty and betrayal. There is no excuse!

I implore YOU, my readers, mothers, fathers, preachers and teachers, elders of the land, Saints to teach our young girls and boys their worth their self-worth. Let us validate them at home; then, they will not look for it in the world. As the Saints of old said, "We need to go back to the old landmark." Teach our children to love themselves. Convey the love of Christ to them and the love He has for them. Teach our children to forgive by forgiving them when necessary. Allow your children to see and hear you pray. Pray with your children and teach them how to pray.

As I entered young adulthood, I tried to cope and maneuver, but as an eighteen-year-old high school drop out with a baby, coupled with emotional and mental ailments, being spiritually bankrupt with no marketable skills, I repeatedly ran into various deterrents and soon those deterrents were replaced by drugs and reckless living. Eventually, I broke and slipped into a deadly state of depression. I fell apart while coming close to a nervous breakdown, but God delivered. I felt life with my true love was rudely interrupted. I found myself nomadically lost, trying to find my way. I was blinded, perplexed, and dumbfounded. The untreated anger kept me at odds with my family, and I was paralyzed with hurt. My heart was aching, I had no smile, and I wanted to die.

Chapter Seven
Loss and Survival

My fiancé was soon discharged, and he settled in the city. As we prepared to execute our plan to marry and move to Missouri, we were excited and happy. We were on our way, hand in hand! Larry bought me another engagement ring. My mother took the one he had originally given me, and I never saw it again.

Meanwhile, I thought Larry had purchased an ARCO gas station between Los Angeles and Inglewood. He was planning to expand after we moved to Missouri, and business was great! We were across the street from the golf course on Western Avenue, where we often took walks.

You will read: "I thought" throughout my book, and that is because I wrote what I thought was true. In researching for this book, I learned a lot of what "I thought" is a lie. Consequently, I am also learning my memories are based and rooted in a pile of lies upon lies upon lies, along with the abuse and other life experiences I have shared.

However, one evening as Larry was closing, he was robbed. During that period, gas stations were full-serve service stations with the cash registers located on the islands. As my fiancé closed out the registers, he was robbed, shot, and killed. I was devastated! To add salt to the wound, my fiancé's mother, sisters, and brothers continued to deny our daughter and denied us the opportunity for closure or to say goodbye.

My world crumbled, and his mother, sisters, and brothers were vicious towards my daughter and me. Recently, my daughter learned her father is buried in Long Beach. Even so, when he died, I died inside, but I had to live, for we had a daughter. The manner in which his family treated my daughter and me was demeaning. I was crushed, and the more scandalous and trifling Deborah became, the more maliciously vindictive I became.

Weekly, we connected, and not once did she ever apologize or take ownership of her niece. Plus, she developed a pious attitude like her mom. I came to realize and accept she was plastic, fake, phony, and a fraud. I had to let her go. She just did not know it yet. The plot thickened, and as I remember how I violated her trust and marriage, I am disgusted. My heart hurts now as I reflect, but at the time, it was my ultimate statement and greatest satisfaction to see her face when she learned of the affair.

To have done that and enjoy it as I did was sick. I was really repulsive, sin-sick. My behaviors and actions were trifling and vindictive, scandalous, malicious, and intended to inflict harm. My mindset was evil. I wanted to go a few rounds with her and run her over with my car. I wanted her to vanish and walk the plank. TKO! I wanted her gone. That was the sickness of the demon that was superimposed upon me. That demon manifested, and I did not like myself, but I accepted who I was at that time.

Years later, I did reach out and ask for forgiveness. We reconciled our differences. I owned up and admitted what I had done, but she NEVER once apologized to me or my daughter. After that, we went our separate ways. When I did my ninth step of the 12 Steps of Alcoholics Anonymous with my sponsor, I let it go and forgave myself.

To this day, our daughter La'Shawn is not allowed to see or speak to her dad's biological father or any other member of the Lusby family. The last report I received, Larry's biological father is alive. He is up in age with failing health. Mr. Hall is his name, and the Lusbys will not permit my daughter to talk to or meet him. He knows of La'Shawn and acknowledges her as his granddaughter. Larry had told him about 'Shawn also. Mr. Hall wants to see La'Shawn. It was being set up, but Deborah got involved and stopped everything.

'Shawn desires to know her roots on her father's side and hopes to gain a glimpse into who her father was. Yet, the repeated repudiation of her desire deeply affects her, and she lives with that hurt. It disquiets my spirit to see my child yearning to know her family and loving the ones who rejects, denies, and dismiss her.

It is so ironic that one of her sons looks so much like Larry. It is astonishing. When my grandson puts on his military uniform, it is like seeing Larry suited up all over again. Although 'Shawn continues to be denied her place in his family and deprived of knowing her lineage through Larry, she prays one day a change of heart will overtake the Lusbys.

Escalated Drug Use

Remember, I told you I smoked my first joint at nine. Well, my drug use escalated. Later, I began taking pills, drinking the Brew, and using other depressants and stimulants. I graduated to ACID (LSD), Jimmy Hendrix, Purple Haze, Orange Sunshine, and White Lighting. Rainbow Paper ACID was the ultimate. That was a period of life where the fog set in, and I began to totally separate myself from everyone, society, and all. As I started isolating, I sank deep into drug use and sales.

As time passed, I learned to navigate through the fog and started dating my first husband Willie B. Sanders. I was going on eighteen, and he was thirty-two. My mom did not care. She was wrapped up with my stepdad who had shot my brother Gilbert. I was in the hospital with a ^{ix}UTI and on May 5, 1971, Willie B. came to the hospital to visit. He brought me something to eat then left.

However, within an hour or so he returned. It was after visiting hours, but he was allowed to see me. Willie informed me that my brother Gilbert had been shot twice. He was in a coma and a full body cast, fighting for his life. I asked where my momma was, and instead of her being by my brother's side, she was bailing her husband out of jail. There was a lot of resentment there. I was ill in one hospital, and Gilbert was shot in another. The next day, on May 6, I turned eighteen and signed myself out. I went straight to the hospital my brother was in and stayed there until he regained consciousness.

Willie B., my daughter, and I waited to see my brother open those hazel/green eyes of his. I needed to hear his voice. Once that was done, I was ready to deal with my mother and her husband on whatever level. We were young, stupid and dumb.

Gilbert told me to leave it alone because he was at fault, so I went to my mother's, packed my daughter's and my belongings, and checked into a motel. Later that month, my boyfriend Willie B. and I eloped to Las Vegas and got married. Upon returning to Los Angeles, we rented a unit in a duplex, off Vernon and Broadway, and that was our first home together.

Life as a Teen Mother and Wife...

Willie B. and I got pregnant, and over the next four years, we had two children of our own: a boy and a girl, and he loved my baby girl, La'Shawn, as his own. Three years later, we purchased a home in the Crenshaw District of Los Angeles. We lived on Bronson Avenue off Santa Barbara Boulevard. For the first eight or nine years, our marriage was wonderful. We were known for our dinner parties, events, holiday dinners, and special occasions. It was Willie B. and me, Little Willie, La'Shawn, Emanuel, and our baby, Laurie. Little Willie was Willie B.'s son with Penny, his first wife. She and I had a good relationship once the dust settled.

Around that time, I enrolled in medical school, studying Surgical Technology. By then, the children were in school, and I was bored. I wanted to make my own money, but I had no skills, I knew how to type, answer phones, book reservations, file, and generate basic business documents and ^{x}PBX. Remember, I dropped out of school in the eleventh grade. But, I always wanted to go into the medical field working in the newborn nursery and neo natal ward.

However, I found a trade school that offered surgical technology with certification, so I enrolled, passed the entrance exam, and was accepted. At graduation, I was the valedictorian and graduated with honors. Upon graduation, I had a job lined up and immediately began my career as a certified surgical technologist (CST).

Unbeknownst to me, that constituted a problem in our marriage. The problem was I had my own income equal to or in excess of his pay rate. During times past, an entry-level Caucasian was paid much more than a long-term Black employee in a supervisorial position.

Willie B. had tenure and was placed in an interim supervisorial position, never moving beyond interim. He was on a higher pay scale than the average employee was but did not earn what an entry-level Caucasian made. Because of the income I generated, he felt challenged or competitive, cheated, or who knows what he felt.

The field of medicine I chose offered me as a new hire just as much as he made with over twenty years seniority working in an interim supervisor's position, and he was the lead machinist as well. Although that was the standard, Willie was paid well, but as time progressed, he changed and started drinking more. He became very controlling, verbally abusive, disrespectful, and belligerent. I soon began to feel threatened and subsequently fell into the category of a battered wife. The titles "victim," "battered-wife syndrome," and "spousal abuse" were not widely used at that time, especially for black women.

Although he was the lead machinist for Seco, a noteworthy company in Santa Monica, the fact remained that he was black. Lockheed eventually hired Willie, and he was paid on a higher scale, demonstrating his worth, regardless of the color of his skin, but by his character and skill level. He was the best.

On the other hand, when he was not at his best, I would go to work with blackened eyes, busted lips, wrenched arms, hanging in a sling and other medical prosthesis I needed after being beaten. But, I went to work and kept my jobs. I was on call three times a week with White Memorial Hospital and held a full-time position with Los Angeles County General Hospital ("General Hospital").

Although times were painfully hard, I endured, tolerating abuse as I prayed for a solution. During that stretch of my life, my two oldest children were in school at Marvin Avenue Elementary where I met the plant manager Craig Dykes. He was very nice, professional, and polite. He opened doors for me and asked me how I was doing, recognizing the anguish in my eyes. We began to talk, and he took an active interest in my children and me, and I in him.

Do not get it twisted. I remained faithful to my husband. However, affections were developing for Craig. Craig was and remains to be an analytical, practical, and a no-nonsense person, just to mention a few of his qualities. Nonetheless, he witnessed the aftermath of the beatings, and I soon noticed Craig getting troubled when I wore dark shades or clothes to cover the bruises. By then, Craig and I were acquaintances. Usually I wore shorts, sandals, and a top, but after the beatings, I had to cover up because I bruise easily. His concern began to concern me, as I did not understand the compassion he was showing. He was concerned about my children's and my wellbeing.

Eventually, my husband hit me again, and that was the last time. I snapped and went into a blackout rage, and that was the end. It was not nice. I fought back; it ended with him severely injured and me with forty-eight stiches in my head. He took an old-school desk telephone to my head. He said I was out-of-control, so he had no choice. "Well, keep your darn hands off me, and you would not have had to make that choice. What do you think?" We then separated and soon divorced.

I began to suffer epileptic seizures. I was in a major car accident on the 110 freeway with my children in the car. I thank God there was no loss of life. Back then, there were no seatbelts in cars. I totaled my car and had to move back home with my mother and her husband.

My, my, my how time passed, but things remained the same for some. The molestation resurfaced, and two of my children were violated as well. One by my mother's husband, and the other by his son, Keith Lambert. I became furious! My children? Herbert/Keith, my children!

When I learned my children were being violated, it was appalling. I immediately went after his son Keith who jumped out the bedroom window. I had blood in my eyes and wanted to kill him. He fled, and I left from over there and rented a room until I could get on my feet and learn to live with epilepsy. I felt completely debased, fierce, hopeless, and dreadfully assaulted. What did I do that was so wrong to deserve all of this?

I sunk into a deeper depression and an inferior personality developed. I felt with men there was always an ulterior motive, and I played on that. My mentality, attitude, and behavior was that of a distressed, angry, vindictive, violent, and promiscuous woman. I was acting wild and dangerous. By then, my stepdad Herbert (Pops), my mother's husband, used to say I looked like death sucking on a soda cracker. But, I did not care. I took on a venomous attitude, one like a mother lion whose cubs had been disturbed by an intruder, and I was on the prowl for Keith Lambert.

Survival

I was a victim of abuse that led to child molestation that led to rape. The abuse led me to accept abuse and degradation as a way of life. However, I overcame that shame and survived. I thank God. But then, my children had to overcome and come to grips with demons that were superimposed upon them by me and my sick family.

I did not know how to [xi]"fight that good fight of faith." I was not taught to pray for my children. In fact, I really did not know how to pray outside of what I heard and the [xii]Sinner's Prayer, the Lord's Prayer. To say the least, I turned away from God, but I knew, I just knew, without a doubt He was with me, and I hid His Word in my heart.

I still had to learn to live with those demons and provide a safe haven and home for my children. By that time, my brother moved into one of the duplexes my mother and stepfather owned. I asked if I could have the second unit, and they agreed. They turned the duplex into a single-family dwelling. So, my brother and I shared the unit, and we had a blast.

We had a group, and we jammed all the time, and all the time, we got high. During one of those jamm sessions I was introduced to crack cocaine. The first time, I turned it down. Then, (there is that "then") I took the pipe, took my time, and tried it. At first, I felt nothing. Then, the guys showed me how it was done, and the next hit was the one. Bam! I was in another world!

After bam, I was hooked. I experienced that first cocaine high...the one addicts chase. After that, I wanted more and more and more. I was already addicted, and I had a high threshold for drugs. I consumed at least twice as much as the average user. It took a lot more for me to get high, and as those of us who have been there knows- that first high, that first hit is what we want to feel again, but we can never get it back.

FYI: One reason it is so difficult for your loved one to stop using he/she is chasing after that first high. He/she wants to erase the pain and escape reality, if only for a moment. What we need you to do, however, is love us. Do not condemn us; love us; do not look down on or talk about us; love us; and most of all, **"Pray for us!"**

Love the addict; hate the addiction. Addiction and alcoholism are medical disorders, diseases listed in the [xiii]Physicians Diagnostic Manuel (PDR). We do not have the enzymes in quantity nor quality to process the drugs and alcohol through our system; therefore, a build-up occurs, resulting in intoxication, euphoria and/or tweaking.

Love even the ones caught in the chronic relapse mode. They can never get that first high back, but they cannot control themselves. They are physically and mentally unable to stop. Untreated, they will use or drink themselves to death. Love them regardless! [xiv]*"Love covers a multitude of sins."* I thank God that I never relapsed. Thank you, Jesus! [xv] *"I can do ALL things through Christ which strengthens me (us)."* He did it for me, and I know He will do it for you, but only [xvi]*God can*, for He is the Almighty!

Back to the story. I was off and running, and I had a new high, and as time went on, I went back to work and got an apartment in the Jungle above Sherm Ally and started selling Angel Dust. Yes, I was smoking it, too. PCP was the thing at that time, for it was an affordable high. With so many people using it, it was becoming more and more popular.

At that time, crack was the rich man's high and PCP, which is a hallucinogen that causes delirium and colorful delusions, hit the scene. At the same time I was selling PCP, I opened two county cases, but I had three. One I was eligible for, and the other two cases were drawn off aliases (assumed identities). Young, determined, making fast paper, and looking for shortcuts, I sold a pound of PCP to an undercover officer. I was the fall guy in a sting.

However, the arresting officer was very kind. He saw my struggle and spoke a good word for me at my trail. However, an investigation was opened, and they found one of my alias accounts. While in prison at Sybil Brand Institute for possession of PCP with intent to sale, I was arrested on one count of county fraud. It is not a good feeling to be in prison serving a one sentence to be arrested on a new charge with the possibility of getting another or increased sentence. That was an indescribable feeling of helplessness, hopelessness, and fright all wrapped in one.

For both charges, I was sentenced to nine months. Both counts were to be served concurrently at Sybil Brand Institute. Because I was married, worked, and had young children, I was allowed to do my time on weekends, in their Work Release Program. My first perception of prison life was that it would be devastating, and at first, it was.

In the end, the experience proved to be a blessing. God turned that bad experience into a good one, and unbeknownst to me, I was on the predestined path for my life. Every weekend, the inmates, guards, cooks, and I had Bible Study, and due to my good behavior, I was released after serving only six months. To my understanding, the Bible Study program remained in place and grew until the prison closed its doors for the last time.

However, regardless of how well things had gone on the inside, upon my release, I elected to celebrate. I went back to the dope house then to the liquor store to get my set-up: a glass pipe, 151 Rum, and the utensil used to consume crack cocaine. Those were the things I did before making it home from prison.

Sadly, it is true, but I thank God for my husband Willie B., who stuck it out with me. At that time, things between us were going well. My going to prison brought us closer, and we worked together as a team for our family's wellbeing. He cared for the children every day and every night over the weekends, as I left home to serve my time at SBI.

Willie and I stayed together for a while longer after I completed the required two years' summary probation. By then, I served my time and was off probation. Willie B. and I were working harmoniously on our marriage until that fight I told you about where he bust me in the head.

Chapter Eight
And the Beat Goes On

Outside of the butt whippings, Willie B. was a good person and a good provider. We drove to Ventura and Oxnard every month to visit his mother and sisters. Those family outings are just a few of the fond memories I shared with Willie. In fact, as I reminisce, Willie B. invented "Road Rage!" I recall being on the road with him and someone may have been going too slowly or cut him off. He would catch up with the person and sling a bottle of Millers Draft or Budweiser out the window and straight into the person's car. Many times, he hit the person with the bottle then dared him/her to pull over. Willie B. spooked those drivers, so they would speed up and take off or slow down and stop at a gas station or on the side of the road until we were out of sight.

Willie was of the ole' school. We called him a Black Mexican. He and his brother Charles were fluent in Spanish. The mindset of some at that time was, "Every once in a while, you gotta slap your woman (wife) around to keep her in place." This destructive behavior continued. One day, as I breastfed my baby, he came over to where I was and slapped me. I was stunned. I had no knowledge what was going on. My first response was to protect my child, so I put her on the couch. By then, he realized what he had done and became apologetic.

But, his slaps graduated to beatings with a closed fist and kicking. Once, he pulled out a machete on me. Then, there came the time I told you about when he hit me, and I flipped the script and went into a blackout rage. I fought back and was hit in the head with the telephone. "OUCH! That hurt!" After the blow to the head, I drove myself to the hospital and ended up with forty-eight stitches under my scalp and in my head. My dad was born with epilepsy, and I was born with the epileptic trait. When Willie hit me in the head, it triggered epilepsy. There are Grand Mal and Petite Mal seizures in epilepsy. The Grand Mal is when the body stiffens and moves with jerk-like motions; those are the ones I had the most.

I learned of the epilepsy shortly after the injury occurred during an accident I had when the children and I were out and about on the Harbor Freeway. It was reported that I allegedly fell asleep behind the wheel of the car, but that was not the case; I had a seizure. Now, I told you I went back home, and being back home with Momz and Pops was like going back in time. Nothing much had changed, and the one thing I did not understand was how Pops sat at the head of the dining room table with a loaded gun (with the safety off), prepared to kill his son for violating my child. He said, "As soon as Keith walks through the door, he is dead!" And, Pops meant it. Remember, he shot my brother Gilbert- twice! So yeah, he was serious. But, there is one thing I don't get: He was willing to kill his son for doing the selfsame thing he had done and continued to do to the children's mother! It puzzles me to this day. Nevertheless, I left Momz because of the continued abuse. Every time thereafter, I rejected him and did not care what he or Momz would say, think or do. I was ready to defend me and mine at all cost.

Also, he took the same gun he sat at the table with, being angry at Keith, and used it to violate one of my children. Then, he abused that same child under knifepoint. After learning all of that and the Keith incident, my children and I moved back to Big Momma's, living in the front house where Big Momma started off.

I had to support my family, so I started working at the Westin Bonaventura Hotel on Figueroa, in Los Angeles. I could no longer work as a surgical technician due to seizures. I lost my certification because the seizures were not yet under control, and I seized during an operation. While at the Bonaventura, I met Steve Henderson, and we were captivated by one another and soon married. That was my second marriage! I wore my mother's wedding dress that was then a soft eggshell white, and Steve wore tails. I tried to recreate Momz and Pops' picture. Three months later, I learned Steve was in a relationship with a man. I quickly kicked him to the curb and annulled the marriage. Thank God, I have a clean bill of health!

Afterwards, I zoned out and went full-blown. In other words, my focus was drugs, and drugs were my focus; I worked to get high and emotionally, I abandoned my children. I kept a roof over their heads and food on the table. For the most part, it was pork and beans and wieners; cold bologna, mayonnaise and bread; Top Ramen; cereal and milk, and fish sticks. That was my grocery list. Do not forget peanut butter and jelly, too! I would leave home on a run and be gone for days.

One day, I was at work, and La'Shawn called me. She decided she wanted to perm her hair. She already had long, silky, and naturally curly hair. She HAD! She called me crying and yelling at the top of her voice, "Momma, my hair is falling out!" I asked her what she did. She told me about the perm, and I asked if she neutralized it. Her answer was, "Neutralize it?" So, I walked her through it, and she neutralized the application. However, when I got home, my baby's hair was shot out. It was gone. Plugs of hair were missing. So, she began wearing wigs and did not like them.

Meanwhile, I escalated to doing things I would not do in my right mind, such as robbery. There were times I would go downtown with another user and rob jewelry stores. I was out of my mind. I carjacked a guy with a toy gun and took his money and car. Another user and I held up dealers, and I did a lot of other stupid things. Thank God, I was covered by the blood of Jesus. The things I did could have caused my death. I was then a full-blown addict in full flight on a never-ending run.

I quit my job and hooked up with a guy in our neighborhood named Norman. And, I ran with motorcycle clubs, but mainly with Pee Wee. He was the president of *Los Angeles Defiant Ones* (LADO), in the 1980s and 90s. I hooked up with some bikers and soon started transporting drugs. I made lots of runs to Arizona, Tijuana, and Mexico. That soon played out as does every other bad thing. I thank God that I never got caught transporting!

Because of my reckless lifestyle, my baby girl Laurie left home at fourteen and had her first child. My son was arrested for grand theft auto, and my oldest held onto my skirt tail no matter what. I took that child to places where there were lots of drugs and undesirables. She was in school and met James Penny. They hooked up and started a family. James was young and into a lifestyle that fed my habit. Daily, I hung around their place, getting high.

Chapter Nine

There is so much more I can tell you about living that lifestyle, and I will, but I want to get down to the reality of my life at that point. The reality of it all is I hit bottom, a low bottom, and continued digging a hole for myself. I was out of control. I continued to hang around my daughters, getting high and getting into situations no daughter should ever see her mother involved in. It was humiliating. I hated myself, but I could not stop.

One day, I went to Norman's, got the motorcycle, and went to Diamond Bar to pick up a package. Three days later, when I returned, there was less than half the package left. That act got me locked up. After socking me a few times, that man locked me in his house. He put some type of barricade up against the front and back doors and secured the windows with nails; then, he left. I was oblivious as to what he was doing and when I tried to leave I could not open the door. So, I tried the window to no avail. However, I busted out a window and ran like a slave being chased by a pack of dogs and trappers! Norman and I soon reconciled and continued to abuse drugs together. It was insane!

Later, I went down to San Julienne to get crack cocaine. San Julienne is in the heart of Skid Row. I went for drugs but stayed to play. That was in 1984. I soon found myself sleeping around Broadway and 16th Street, under the 10 Freeway, in my cardboard condo. I had the latest model automobile, a V8-Shopping Cart-1900 SE series, and I was hustling my way through my habit. I did things no sane woman would subject herself. Nonetheless, I did them. I was an official resident of Skid Row.

I hustled pallets, cans, bottles, cooper, stainless steel, men, and plastic. I made false social security cards and IDs and laundered counterfeit money. I found myself in possession of a money order machine and blank money orders, so I ran counterfeit money orders, too. I opened bank accounts and ran checks through them. I created payroll and personal checks with valid account and routing numbers. I did what I had to do for that next high. I operated under the "no morals" clause of the streets. 'They do not care so why should I?; I gotta get them before they get me'- that sort of thinking. The thing about all this is I was never comfortable with such behavior. I messed up a lot. I darn near got myself killed, and I did get caught. The adversary planted seeds in an already seared conscience where thoughts of death and destruction were prevalent, but he could not keep me in that foul and toxic state of mind.

While on Skid Row, I lived the life of a vagrant. I began to wander and lived from mission to mission. I walked the streets from sunset to sunrise. On rainy nights, I would ride the bus from the beginning of the line to the end, and that continued for many years. There are times of the month when times on the Skids gets hard and dangerous more so than usual. Between the 30th and the 5th, it became treacherous. Dog-eat-dog brashness emerges or you are befriended by those who on the average dodge you, but when the money comes, everyone is your friend and in your face. These are the dates the Skid Row population gets their benefits, and they become prey for the slaughter. But, I thank God. Through Jesus and by His Holy Ghost, He hid me under His Mighty Wings of Protection. Seven years later, I made it over. He lifted me and took me off the Skids.

One evening, I was at Union Rescue Mission waiting for dinner. As I waited, a rat, the size of a cat, ran across my feet, and that was it. I HATE RODENTS! I jumped out of my seat like it was hot and on fire. That is when I heard the voice of God tell me, "This is not what I created you for." That was winter of 1991. In Spring 1992, I walked into Union Station Pasadena (U.S.P.) seeking help, and that is where I remained for 111 days. Let me tell you a little something about that.

    U.S.P. is a homeless shelter that focuses on mainstreaming the displaced, addict, the co-dependent, disenfranchised, and families back into life on life terms. The terms of life I had to come to grips with is I have no life without Jesus Christ. Left to my own devices, I failed to live the life that was predestined for me. But, U.S.P. has a wide referral base, and they offered the "spiritual" support and guidance I needed to find my "spiritual self." Also through their vast resources and opportunities, women with children and families are and continue to be blessed and given another chance in life through Euclid Villa and the Women's Program. Union Station provides hope for the hopeless and the addict. They offer recovery through places like Acton and Warm Springs.

    One of U.S.P. requirements is residents are to attend the daily mandated noon meeting of Alcoholics Anonymous held at the shelter, and there I would sit at the table with my Bible, refuting everything they were saying and knocking down their axioms. I would turn to a passage in scripture, read it to them, and start witnessing. I quickly gained the nickname "Preacher D."

    One evening, I could not sleep. I was grieving the loss of my eighteen-month-old grandson. The night counselor, whom we called Uncle Henry, gingerly asked me to put my Bible down and pick up the Big Book of Alcoholics Anonymous. (God rest his soul.) He told me once I understood the principles and concepts of the twelve-step process, I could pick up my Bible and have a spiritual balance. He said I would also learn how to apply Biblical principles in all of my affairs. I did that, but it was very hard for me because I was a "religious person." I surely was. I was a religious addict, active sinner, and scattered like sheep. However, as I learned to apply Biblical principles in all I did and said my deliverance came. On April 2, 2017, I celebrated 25 years of quality and sobriety. Thank you, Jesus.

While at U.S.P., we were assigned a counselor. Gilbert Nelson was mine; however, before it was over, all three counselors had me cornered. I was so lost, hurt, and bewildered. When I grieve, I grieve hard- as noted when my granddaddy passed in 1955. My baby girl Laurie's eighteen-month-old son never awoke from his nap. Emotionally, I was a wreck, and at that meeting, I gave into sweet surrender. That was the closest I had ever come to relapse. I thank God for the people He put in my life at that time.

I felt helpless. I could not take the pain from my baby. However, I am not Jesus. Only Christ can and does bear our pains. Laurie's grief of losing her son was unbearable, and I know this because my baby shut down for a minute. I had never seen my baby in such a state. She grieved hard but silently. All the while, the Lord had her cradled in His arms, and He hid her under His Mighty Wings of Protection, too. My God! Laurie was and still is *STRONG!* Laurie is a blessed child, and she grew to be strong in the Lord and the power of His Might! R.I.P. Lil' Antoine. GranE loves you more every day, always in my heart.

The only way I was able to stand was by the grace of God, prayer, and every evening going back to U.S.P. before dark. Also, I protected myself and newly-found freedom in Christ by bringing someone who had time with me, and it worked. I did not feel confident enough to stay anywhere during the night, except U.S.P. Anyone who has experienced a life of addiction knows night is when *"the creeps come out!"* Night is when demons become more active as well, especially in the wee hours of the morning when they are trying to plant seeds in our subconscious minds as we sleep and lay in sweet slumber. As we enjoy our dreams and the inertia of comfort, the enemy and his demonic armies are out to get us any way they can! And, I was fighting to stay sober and refused to subject myself to the demons' temptation of cocaine. It was in the night when I did most of my dirty work, and I was still healing and being delivered, so I made sure I was in a safe and drug-free environment when night fell.

Do not think it was easy for me, not for a moment; it was not easy at all. One hundred and eleven days later, I completed the program and mainstreamed into managing Sober Living facilities. That worked until it did not. I was what is called a "dry drunk." I then took on jobs at sober living facilities to becoming a housemother at Casa Maria, a transitional housing for women with children. I messed that up. Although I was sober, my behaviors were still the same.

I stole my co-worker's food stamps. And the woman called the police (rightfully so), and I was busted. Over some funky food stamps, I lost my position, and that landed me living from pillar to post, but I did not get high. That is when I started working at Union Rescue Mission. The same dark mission the Lord called me out of into His marvelous Light. He sent me back as an employee.

By then, I had acquired a car and was sleeping in it. A co-worker saw me and inquired what was going on. I shared my plight with her, and to my surprise, she was my supervisor. She provided me a room upstairs at the mission and allowed me to stay there for ninety days. I appreciated what she did for me, and my hope was being restored. I sought help for myself because I still had no coping skills and the lacked basic skills needed to be responsible. For example, I did not know how to balance a check book or how to create a budget and follow it. I was not taught that. I was taught "if you have it, spend it, so the women coming behind you won't have anything to get." I worked at URM for three to four years until an opportunity came my way that I could not refuse. Apple One Temporary Services located in the South Bay area offered me a position and a career opportunity.

The skills I acquired down through the years were paying off. They were in demand, and I was sent all over the South Bay area automating offices. Computers were becoming affordable to the average business owner, and there arose a need for systematizing. I was well trained in that field, and that position provided me a well-paying job for the City of Long Beach.

I was blessed with a one-bedroom apartment in Gardena, CA, overlooking the swimming pool. One morning about 3 a.m., there was a knock at my door. Like Madea (Tyler Perry), I opened the door with my 9-mm, ready to protect myself. Remember, I told you about being robbed in my home? So, yeah. I was ready. It was the Department of Children and Family Services (DCFS) standing at my door with four of my grandchildren. They had been removed from their father's home in Pomona and became statistics of the system. I took my babies. No stranger will raise any of my children as long as I am able bodied and the blood is still running warm in my veins!

I worked with my daughter, their father, and DCFS, to try to return custody to their mother. The father went to his parenting classes, took random drug tests, and passed. The courts returned the children to him. Within three months, DCFS was knocking at my door again. Again, I took them in. That happened a total of four times. However, on the fourth time, I would not allow the children to cross my threshold without the worker agreeing to put a permanent plan in place. I could no longer do that every three to six months.

They placed the children with me under Long-Term Foster Care. That was effective for one to two years. When the Long-Term Foster Care contract was about to expire, the children were to be put up for adoption. The father's parental rights had been terminated, and because my daughter did not meet the requirements, her parental rights were terminated as well. The children were legally in my care, and the Long-Term Foster Care Contract expired. Without hesitating, I adopted the children with their permissions. The children did not want to leave, and they had lived with the fear of being taken from me. The adoption gave them closure and peace knowing they were safe and regarded as my children, so they took on the last name "Wesson." However, I insisted they become "Penny/Beasley Wessons" and they agreed.

Then, their mother (my daughter) and my mother teamed up and turned against me. I would not turn the children over to their mother. I told her she could spend as much time with them as she liked. I was even willing for them to stay with her and go to school. We did not live that far apart, so I was willing. Vacations or whenever and for however long we decided, the children could stay with her. That was not good enough. She wanted her children back and rightfully so. She is their mother! She had a right to want them back; however, under the circumstances, I was being monitored for a few years by DCFS.

I opened my doors to my daughter, and I wanted her to have them back, but she failed to meet their requirements, and I was under the magnifying glass. No one wanted to hear my side. They just wanted me to turn over the children *and* the checks, but I would not. I was concerned about the children and myself. If I did what they wanted me to do and was caught, the children would go back into the system, and I could have been charged with child endangerment. That was one of the most horrific experiences I have ever had with my family.

It was my daughter, mother, and all the children (about fourteen total) that went to DCFS and filed bogus reports against me. The family had to come together before a mediator. I was accompanied by my psychologist, a friend, an associate, and my pastor, so there were five of us. As I think about what happened, I am saddened. Saddened to know one of my children did that to me. But, all is forgiven, and all is well! I love that little girl so much, and I thank God for her, but tensions grew, so I walked away.

On the other hand, the father had gang relations and sent us through lots of changes, and I reported the offenses to our worker. The worker mandated me to move immediately because the father had found out where we lived. They gave me fourteen days, or they were going to place the children in protective custody. So, we moved to Hawthorne. The children were doing well; they were thriving. As time marched on, there was a fire at the children's school, and it made the evening news. Little to my surprise, my grandson Edward (Penny) was one of the children interviewed.

Their father saw Penny on the news and was at the school the following day. He followed Penny home, and the cycle repeated itself. I followed procedure and contacted our worker. Again, we had to move, so we did. Shortly after that incident, we were assigned a new worker, and upon her initial visit to the father, she gave him our new address. That evening, I received a call from DCFS stating our confidentiality had been compromised, and we had to move. That time, they assisted me in moving, but they watched me like a hawk because of boggish reports.

It was difficult being under the Department of Children and Family Services' microscope and consciously having to avoid the children's father daily. Then, there was the anger of the children's mother and my mom. My God! The children were having their own personal issues. Weekly, they were in therapy, training, or having to go and do something. In addition, they suffered from contentions within the family. and lo and behold, [xvii]Post Traumatic Stress Disorder (PTSD) manifested, and it was four of them! It was hard!

Constantly moving took its toll on me. I was livid from having to move again. Within seventy-two hours, the children and I moved to Lancaster, CA, where for the second time, our confidentiality was compromised. DCFS was training new field workers, and a woman came to our home for an annual assessment. Later that evening, I received a call from DCFS, stating our confidentiality was compromised again, and I had to move. However, due to the circumstances, I was granted emergency Section 8. That calmed me down quite a bit! A whole heck of a lot. That time, I moved to California City.

For the first couple of years, I drove to and from work to the City of Long Beach. Also, every Sunday, I drove to church in L.A. I blew two automobile engines, I eventually took a job with LAC and worked as a timekeeper at High Desert Hospital in Lancaster. My God, the children and I went through so much, and "together" we made it. Guys, you are the best!

After adopting my grandchildren, by the request of their mother, I started being accused of selfishness, greed and for being overly protective. Well, with my past who wouldn't be? And, the toxic reasoning, whenever I told an adult what happened, they would make excuses or say, "It didn't happen like that," or "I'm sure he was just playing around with you. You like to be tickled, don't you?" That was their rationalization: "I like to be tickled." Sick!

I was not so young that I did not know what was happening. I was in a bra, beginning to develop. Secondly, my uncle and/or male cousin should not have been playing with me or any other minor male or female like that! I was also told I am too suspicious, I overthink, and I embellish the truth. Yeah, right!

As a child, trusting the adults in my life, who were obligated and mandated by God to be my protectors, resulted in me being repeatedly violated! As an adolescent, I was awkward, shy, subdued, and smoking dope (as my mother says). As a young adult, further traumatized, debased and abused, I withdrew even more. I was on a downward spiral, spiraling to an early grave, but God by His Son Jesus, through the Holy Ghost, saved me.

As an immature adult, the molestation resurfaced, and two of my children were violated by family as well. "No more!" The buck stops here. As a mature adult, I refuse to be a victim and will protect the innocence of our children. That curse has been broken in our family. None of my great-grandchildren (to my knowledge) have been violated. To God be the glory. There have not been any teen pregnancies in our family for nearly two decades. To God be the glory. God is good, and He will be just as good to you as He is to me. I am no better than you, so enter into the sheepfold.

This is not the end. In fact, it is only the beginning. However, if you identify with my story, I want you to know, you are not alone. There are many of you relating to my story, and there are many suffering and hurting right now, just as I was. "No more!" "Suffer no more!" "Hurt no more!" "No more!"

If you made it to this point, then this is your season. It is *your* time to rise up and fulfill *your* Divine destiny, and there is a Divine purpose for *you* in God's Kingdom! It is time for *you* to heal and be delivered! It is time to uncover and discover who *you* are in Christ! *You* need to know that *you* are valued, loved, and respected. *You* deserve a chance to… [xviii]"*live life and live it more abundantly.*" Our Father in heaven is waiting on *you*, so let Him in. He will elevate *you* to the next level; only God can do that for *you*.

Your vice may not be drugs. You may be a sex addict, an overeater, co-dependent, a gambler, or have another vice you cannot control. There are so many vices around us today disguised to be fun, entertaining, a legit fast money-making opportunity, or some other vice, that once in its grip, it will lock onto you and seize you like a vice grip, and it will not let you go! It will not be easy to get out of its grips either. You will need help to release it, or you *will* be consumed and perish.

But, there is a way out. I do not know who your god is, and all I ask is you give God a chance. Ask the god you serve to direct you to the Truth. [xix]"The Truth shall make (set) you free."

Words to inspire, convert, convict, and arrest one's attention to the All Powerful One:

PRAY

Learn to pray for yourself. You may say, "I don't know how to pray." I have included [xx]"God's Chair," a poem I love to read. You can start there and talk to God the same way you talk to others, except with reverence and thanksgiving. Please, no vulgarity. You are intelligent, and you have been blessed to have a vocabulary.

Know there *IS* help for you. You do not stand alone, **but** *YOU* must take the first step, because it starts with **YOU**!

- It is time for a new beginning. You *deserve* another chance and a fresh start!
- Uncover, discover, and face your fears with Jesus at your side, and experience newfound freedom and hope!
- Trust God. [xxi]He will walk through it with you and bring you out on the other side, and you won't even smell like smoke, like the three Hebrew boys in the fiery furnace who came out without being singed or burned.
- He is ready. Are you? Let Jesus Christ be your Chief Cornerstone and [xxii]"set your affections on things above."
- Give your heart to Jesus!!! Build your hope on [xxiii]"things eternal."
- Let your foundation begin and end with God and God alone.

PLEASE: Do not get discouraged, angry, or turned-off because I suggest you try God. I am not pushing my beliefs. However, I tried God for myself, and He **delivered** me from cocaine, all mind-altering substances, and the grip Satan had on me. In twenty-five years, I have had NO desire to go back. I have been blessed beyond my wildest dreams, and He will do the same for you and more! I know I will not go back. The world "recovers."

God's people are "DELIVERED." There is a big difference in the two.

In the Mighty name of Jesus, I pray, you will come [xxiv]"...to believe, that a Power greater than ourselves (you) could restore us (you) to sanity." LORD, show these your readers the straight path to deliverance and salvation as you lead them down the path of righteousness. I say to you, man, woman, boy or girl try God, and, that is all I ask. This, Lord, is your servant's prayer. In your name Jesus, it is done! †Amen

God bless us all!
Dr. D.

God's Chair

A man's daughter had asked the local pastor to come and pray with her father. When the pastor arrived, he found the man lying in bed with his head propped up on two pillows and an empty chair beside his bed.

The pastor assumed that the old fellow had been informed of his visit. "I guess you were expecting me," he said. "No, who are you?" "I'm the new associate at your local church," the pastor replied. "When I saw the empty chair, I figured you knew I was going to show up." "Oh yeah, the chair," said the bedridden man.

"Would you mind closing the door?" Puzzled, the pastor shut the door. "I've never told anyone this, not even my daughter," said the man. "But all of my life I have never known how to pray. At church, I used to hear the pastor talk about prayer, but it always went right over my head. I abandoned any attempt at prayer," the old man continued, "until one day about four years ago my best friend said to me, 'Joe, prayer is just a simple matter of having a conversation with Jesus.

Here's what I suggest: Sit down on a chair; place an empty chair in front of you, and in faith see Jesus on the chair. It's not spooky because he promised, "I'll be with you always." Then just speak to him and listen in the same way you're doing with me right now.' So, I tried it and I've liked it so much that I do it a couple of hours every day. I'm careful, though. If my daughter saw me talking to an empty chair, she'd either have a nervous breakdown or send me to off to the funny farm."

The pastor was deeply moved by the story and encouraged the old guy to continue on the journey. Then he prayed with him, and returned to the church.

Two nights later the daughter called to tell the pastor that her daddy had died that afternoon.

"Did he seem to die in peace?" he asked. "Yes, when I left the house around two O'clock, he called me over to his bedside, told me one of his corny jokes, and kissed me on the cheek.

When I got back from the store an hour later, I found him dead. But there was something strange, in fact, beyond strange…really weird! Apparently, just before Daddy died, he leaned over and rested his head on a chair beside the bed."   -author unknown

List of References

[i] Words such as "Hell," Damn," and "Ass," are words found in the Official King James Version (KJV) of the Holy Bible and are not used in a profane manner. These words are used to indicate the depth and gravity of each statement in which it is used.

[ii] Tweaking is an act observed of cocaine users. They crawl around on the carpet picking up everything white that look like it could be crack cocaine. They bite, burn or taste whatever they pick up to see if it is in fact cocaine. They become hypervigilant and paranoid, constantly looking through peepholes and windows and they are easily spooked.

[iii] 2 Corinthians 12:9 KJV [9] And he said unto me, My grace is sufficient for thee: for my strength is made perfect in weakness. Most gladly therefore will I rather glory in my infirmities, that the power of Christ may rest upon me

[iv] *A Charge to Keep I Have*, Wesley, Charles (1762)

[v] Watts, Isaac "Old Dr. Watts" 1719, I Love the Lord, He Heard My Cry

[vi] Gershwin, George 1935, Porgy and Bess

[vii] The Diagnostic and Statistical Manual of Mental Disorders, Fifth Edition (DSM-5) is the 2015 update to the American Psychiatric Association's (APA) classification and diagnostic tool. In the United States, the DSM-5 serves as a universal authority for psychiatric diagnosis. DSM-5 Wikipedia, the free encyclopedia http://www.en.wikipedia.org/wiki/DSM-5

[viii] Boones Farm Apple Valley wine mixed with THC. *We extracted the THC and mixed content with Boones Farm Apple or Strawberry Wine: end product: "Vietnam Brew."*

[ix] Urinary Tract Infection - A urinary tract infection, or UTI, is an infection of the urinary tract. The infection can occur at different points in the urinary tract. However, I had an "complete" UTI, my entire urinary tract was involved.

[x] Today 2017, PBX is defined as a *private branch exchange*, a private telephone switchboard. In the 80's and 90's when I was a PBX Operator, dial "0" for operator it was identified as a Public Broadcasting Exchange. The system I worked on was one of the first renovated PBX systems marketed. It is a plug-in console with a CRT terminal and lead cords.

[xi] 1 Timothy 6:12 Fight the good fight of faith, lay hold on eternal life, whereunto thou art also called, and hast professed a good profession before many witnesses.

[xii] Matthew 6:9-13 After this manner therefore pray ye: Our Father which art in heaven, Hallowed be thy name. Thy kingdom come. Thy will be done in earth as it is in heaven. Give us this day our daily bread. And forgive us our debts, as we forgive our debtors. And lead us not into temptation, but deliver us from evil. For thine is the kingdom, and the power, and the glory, forever. Amen.

[xiii]Physicians Diagnostic Manuel (PDR). We do not have the enzymes in quantity nor quality to process the drugs and alcohol through our system; therefore, a build-up occurs, resulting in intoxication or what we call [xiii]"tweaking."

[xiv] - 1 Peter 4:8 And above all things have fervent **charity** among yourselves: for charity shall cover the multitude of sins.

> Charity (chaŕ-i-ti)-when translated is (agape), agape translates into (LOVE) therefore, charity equates into love and love is spoken of as the greatest of the three Christian graces (1Corinthians 12:31-13:13). ... In the King James Version in 26 places from 1 Corinthians onward use the same Greek word.

[xv] Philippians 4:13 I can do all things through Christ which strengtheneth me

[xvi] Graves, Frank, gospel Give *Me My Flowers*, 2003

[xvii] PTSD is a disorder commonly found in veterans and Military Personnel. However, PTSD, is also common amongst the abused, molested, rape, and/or victims of violent crimes as well as witness'. PTSD is defined as: According to mental health professionals, post-traumatic stress disorder (or PTSD) is a mental condition that results in a series of emotional and physical reactions in individuals who have either witnessed or experienced a traumatic event.

[xviii] John 10:10: The thief cometh not, but for to steal, and to kill, and to destroy: I am come that they might have life, and that they might have *it* more abundantly.

[xix] John 8:32 And ye shall know the truth, and the truth shall make you free

[xx] God's Chair, Author unknown

[xxi] Hebrew 13:5, "...*be* content with such things as ye have: for he hath said, I will never leave thee, nor forsake thee. Matthew

28:20 ...lo, I am with you always, even unto the end of the world. Amen.

[xxii] Colossians 3:2, Set your affection on things above, not on things on the earth.

[xxiii] 2 Corinthians 4:18, While we look not at the things which are seen, but at the things which are not seen: for the things which are seen are temporal; but the things which are not see *are* eternal.

[xxiv] Wilson, William G. (Bill), 2nd edition, Alcoholic Anonymous (AA), (Big Book of) 1955

You may reach Dr. Wesson for speaking engagements at the following email: authorwessonLMLIOL@gmail.com

www.ingramcontent.com/pod-product-compliance
Lightning Source LLC
Chambersburg PA
CBHW070325100426
42743CB00011B/2563